DISCOVERY
IN
PRAYER

DISCOVERY
IN
PRAYER

ROBERT J. HEYER, S.J.
RICHARD J. PAYNE

Editorial Assistants:
Robert Bueter, S.J.
John Kirvan, C.S.P.
Charlotte Baecher

Designed by
Emil Antonucci

Photographed by
Edward Rice

PAULIST PRESS
New York, N.Y. / Paramus, N.J. / Toronto, Ont.

DISCOVERY
IN
PRAYER

CONTENTS

INTRODUCTION

"Can Modern Man Pray?" This central religious question of our day was asked and explored in a recent Time Magazine article (December 30, 1968). Jaroslav Pelikan, a Yale theologian, replied that "in a time of frenetic Christian activity, when everybody is busy solving the problems of the world, prayer must seem to be, at the least, a luxury item."

It is within the critical context of modern man, who feels little need of God's help, that young men and women are awakening to the meaning, need, and experience of personal prayer. Often, like the person in "I Am a Rock" who decides that poetry and books can replace his need for friendship, this need for personal religion is smothered in young people who have come to see prayer as childish and magical, as meaningless and a sign of weakness.

There is a certain rhythm in the process of religious growth. A person moves from a "magical" religion through a legal one to a fully personal religious experience. At first, God is a Santa Claus who gives gifts, a Superman who can do anything, an old Father Time. Magical expressions surround the realities of sacraments, sin, prayer. Grace is a green stamp issued to trade in for heaven, and prayer is a self-centered "gimme." Slowly a person learns to say "Thank You!" But understanding and freely living these words requires more time. He becomes pre-occupied with legalisms and sees God as a Judge, as one who condemns and rewards him for keeping the rules. Prayer becomes the repetition of memorized formulae, recited at meals and before bed. A personal religion develops when God is seen as a Friend. In a relationship founded on love, prayer becomes a deeply personal communication— the mature Christian shares his hopes, anxieties, concerns, disappointments and needs with a Friend. The magic and legal levels gradually find their authentic mystery and responsibility in this personal religious growth.

If this growth process is frustrated, the person will remain on a magicial or legal level of religious practice. Too often, religious formation in the communities—family, school, church— consists in evoking mainly magical and legal responses. Fostering personal religious experience is not an easy task, yet it is an important one. A person who is concerned with fostering religious maturity will assist them intelligently and give them opportunities to search freely.

This book offers a wide selection of prayers, personal reflections, and photography which attempt to initiate a search for personal prayer in the events of his everyday life. They also attempt to evoke a recognition of Christ present and revealing in life's experiences. Discovery in Prayer is intended for personal reflection and communal prayer. These prayers might also be used as part of the liturgy and as retreat reflections.

COMMUNICATION

The thing is that we have words to hear,
and hands that touch.
So why don't they seem enough?
Why all the silence? Why all this distance?
What I want is that I should know you,
and you, me.
And the *others*
To pass beyond and beneath the "otherness"
of us all.
But not to lose our selves.
To stretch between the mystery of mutual
and irreducible "I's."
To communicate, which means (and this
the dictionary says is "archaic") to
share.
Not archaic, just hard.
Hard because we have ultimately to live
with the silences, and the distances,
with "I" as "I" and "you" as "you".
And go on stretching.
Go on trying. Putting into words. Touching.

You are an open letter about Christ written not
with pen and ink but with the Spirit of the Living
God. The message has been engraved, not in stone
but in living men and women.

2 Corinthians 3:2-3

SOMEHOW
I
DIDN'T
KNOW

somehow
  i didn't know
    about the humanity of man
  although i'd heard about it
    often enough
  from the local very reverend
    and his very local peers
  and a garrulous grayhaired history teacher
    with rouge on her cheeks
  not to mention
    several presidents
      and my barber george
till the other day
  i saw a young mexican boy
    with dirty ankles
  waiting beside his sixty year old father
    in the
      unemployment compensation line

John Atherton

*"Humanity" is so vague, so cold, so unreal—and yet
it stands in every unemployment line, it slumps
drunkenly and plays gloriously in every park, and
it runs in fear and joy and climbs in search and
flight and falls dead, tired, and satisfied in every
city in the world. "God" is so vague, so cold, so
unreal—and yet. . . . Do I see Him? Do I hear
Him? Do I want to?*

TIED UP

Jesus, I want to say lots of things to you
And tell you how I feel
And it feels kinda silly
Talking to someone you don't see.

I'm kinda all tied up inside of me
And here's a hope you will help me
Get untied.

I'm even afraid that somebody is going to
Laugh at me and poke fun at me
And call me some kind of a creep.
I wish I could feel that I could trust you.

Carl Burke

*That's the trouble—Jesus can't be trusted: He
knows too much, He will ask too much. But only
He knows enough to straighten me out, only He
will ask enough to make me live. Why am I afraid?*

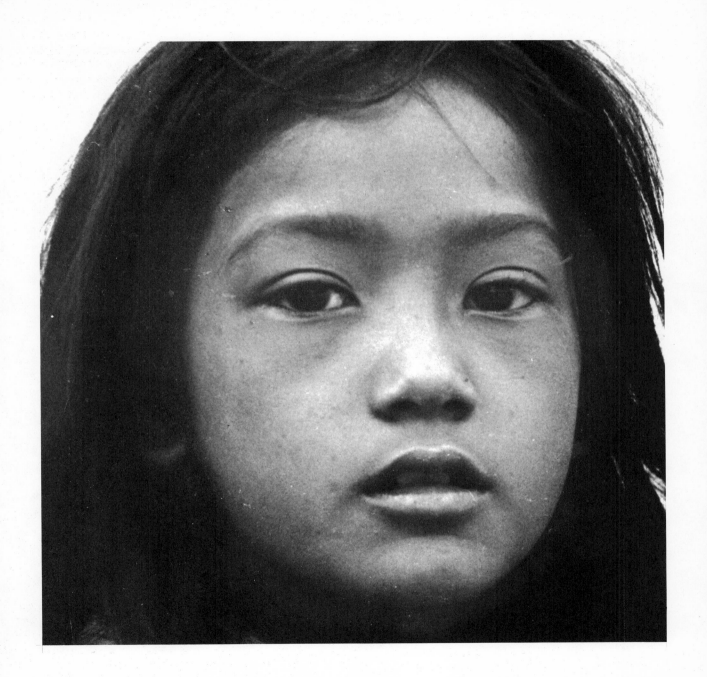

TO WHOM DO YOU PRAY?
TWO STUDENT VIEWS

"Ever since grammar school I have relied heavily upon my patron saint for aid in guiding my life. I dealt with him as a person who once walked within this same world in which I now live. I consider him as almost an older brother to look up to for guidance. But most of all since entering high school and learning the true value of Christ as a "Person" I now rely on Him most of all. I find myself talking to Him in a language simple and seemingly prayless language. I don't know if some people consider this right or wrong but I find myself doing nothing but asking God for this and for that. I realize that this is being very selfish and now I try to ask this Person to give me the courage and strength to do my best at all times. I try now to pray, not for my own selfish gains, but to get to know Christ on a more intimate basis and to ask that I profit the 'guy next door' rather than myself."

"I sort of have two ways of praying. One is formally to God—the usual stuff like 'Our Fathers' and Acts of Faith etc. This takes place sometimes at night but mostly at Mass. I have no better reason for this than habit. The other is straight to Jesus, or whoever the guy is who keeps bugging me —like a good friend bugs y'to do what's right. I forget about him a lot but I keep in touch a few times during the day—maybe when I'm writing or I get psyched or I'm lonely or everything is getting bitchy. This is when I really pray, and I guess I do it because I think this Jesus loves me—and that's no crap, either. Who better can a person talk to than someone he knows isn't going to be petty and give him a hard time. And besides, I think I love Jesus—or at least I'm getting to love him."

This is a good question because as of right now I don't know whom I'm praying to. If I do pray, it is to hopefully clear up any of these very same questions. Right now I'm at a point where I just don't know if God exists but I'm willing to give it a try.

I pray to God the Father, Jesus Christ, and the Blessed Virgin, but mostly to Jesus Christ. I pray because I've been brought up to pray, because I need things, because I'm insecure, because I want to thank God.

Four views—well, why not a fifth . . . mine? But maybe I pray too little . . . or too much? But I might be wrong . . . yet may be right? Well, world, here it is: my own personal, solitary, individual view! I pray to. . . .

QUESTION
TO CHRIST

on waking up at three

WHO ARE YOU, YOU WHO WALK
not from history into a legend
but through history into death to abide
and ask me who I am?
Who are you, who can you be?
Certainly you are alone in this,
beating on history with your question,
the question you are, the question of you,
the question we wrestle over, you and I, each trying
to pose it:

Who are you, beating with your question on the
doors of history

till they admit you into death
there to abide beyond question?
Who are you and what is this question
that comes back at me?

You are a king then, that's right is it,
you don't deny that, but what do you affirm?

O we've been through all this so many times
(and we do it all the time to each other)
it gets us nowhere until we killed you and then
the whole massive determined accurate
one way movement of history
pointed you at my heart:
the Roman spear of history
entering the heart of the user and making him
useless, speechless, kings stand speechless before
you.

Who can you be, how can you be
who seem to break the law of being,
the law of convincing seeming,
you who are darkly man and come upon me
with flesh I cannot deny, you who never answer
but make all flesh your answer?
Man of the dark way, finding your shape in death
where all for us is shapeless; who then are you
who marry the contradiction of life
to the horrid nonsense of death
making the accurate shape of man
which I cannot touch O God who are you?

There is only one way,
that's you all over only one way;
there's only one way for all of us
leading to death, but for you
death was itself the way.

Impossibly accurate man
aimed by your Trial which stood you
before your questioners with death behind you.
That is the pattern of every capital trial,
but normally the pattern is loose
with the Prisoner casting around for ways of escape;
but with yours the pattern is tight
yet not because you plead guilty; you don't,
the pattern tightens because you do not plead guilty
but force upon your accusers
a verdict you don't accept:
and while you don't accept the verdict
you accept the sentence as part of a logic
which only you seem to understand;
and this it is that tightens the pattern beyond our
                                    comprehension,

for in this logic of yours,
not spun out of your head
but brought to birth by you out of the situation,
the court is surprised into universal human meaning,
becomes the human race in council
and says, for man, that death is the only way:
and that is the extraordinary thing,
that is the thing that flattens the mind
to an unbearable simplicity;
that men who, as men, know always that death is
the only way,

find themselves in a court pronouncing that as a
sentence.
It's almost as though these men,
not just representative of the common run of
humanity
but representing it,
had to pronounce on the big life stood in their
midst,
the Kingdom, the Big Country,
and said quite correctly 'it cannot be in this world'
and so enacted. They couldn't put a foot wrong:
whether pronounced in malice or in pragmatism or
as metaphysical statement,
'it cannot be in this world' enacts your death.
And thus the undoubted realism of the proceedings
is constantly on the verge of becoming theology:
and that again is you all over and is why I lose you
and pursue you and get caught.

Neither murder nor suicide nor a straight judicial
sentence,
none of the ways to death,
but the uniquely political event
compounded of you and us
fixes you forever our Judge.

Who would ever have thought it,
who ever would have thought you could be so
serious?

Least of all—my God yes least of all–
me who have preached you
and have never doubted or tried you,
we who are invested in you
and sell you as a harmless academic exercise.
Now I begin to see that he who would truly preach
you
must crucify you again, expose you again
to the bitter twisting winds and minds of men,
set up again with brutal realism the court that
condemned you;
and now I find myself actually hesitating,
such is your terrible maturity,
to burst you upon our time.

One thing is clear:
the point will be reached when the discontent of
the young
will be, to their great surprise, thrusting you before
their superiors,
making them your judges, yes they from whose
minds and lips you are never absent.
It will come, if you are you it will come:
there is absolutely no other way
forward no other way.
And thus we shall all of us make for the great death
in our midst,
the death we create by not loving and fear to
examine,
and there we shall have our answer,
there alone, in these bloody espousals
Christ we make you.

Sebastian Moore

*I knew it. I no sooner talk to You than You get
serious—maturity, death, and bloody espousals. I
tried to hide behind my questions and rest in my
doubts, but You answer with a question that puts
me on the spot. But I know it, all too well I know it*
*"forward no other way." So I'll ask you and
even while asking You I know You ask me: "Will
You help me?"*

POSSIBILITY

Possibility must begin with dialogue, which is more
than the freedom to speak. It is the willingness
to listen, and to act.

Robert F. Kennedy

*Am I possible? I'm ready to speak, I'm even trying
to listen; but will I act?*

HOW ABOUT YOUR GOD?

When someone starts believing for good,
when he starts taking God seriously once for all,
he usually begins by scandalizing everybody:
all those "good Christians" who are too "humble"
to depart from the accepted pattern;
all those who feel they have the right religion—
a time-honored one that jolts nobody.

Take Saint Paul, for example,
when he was persecuting the Christians.
He thought he had the right religion.
None was more cognizant of its commands than he,
none more zealous in having them carried out.
He'd become furious with people
who were forever questioning everything
and who seemed to think
some matters hadn't been definitively settled yet.
"After all," he reasoned, "we have the Law.
Everything's been foreseen and legislated.
Let's not have any of these innovations!"
He was a strict observer of complete orthodoxy.

Still, when this thoroughly religious man
finally and really met the God
he thought he was serving,
he was thunderstruck
and gasped, "Who-who are you?"
The God he'd so fiercely clung to had hardened
    into an idol.

How about our God,
the one we think we're serving?
Is He the tender,
solicitous,
responsive,
persecuted—
and, therefore, persecutable—being
who revealed Himself to Saint Paul?
Or is He some almighty, remote bookkeeper
who'll catch us the next time around
if our accounts aren't in order?
Many Christians wouldn't want to be the God
they've fabricated:
they'd be more likeable than that!

When Jesus revealed Himself
and, consequently, the Father
(for "he who sees Me sees the Father also"),
we discovered, first of all, that God's infinitely better
than we'd imagined.
He's near us,
benevolent,
young and gay,
companionable and loving.
He begs for our friendship:
if we wander away from Him,

Louis Evely

Thank You, God, for Jesus. I need a friend, a companion along the way because I'm possible and I'm

going to act and they won't like it. They didn't like Paul, and they didn't like Abraham, Martin, and John; but they forgot to ask: Did You?

TRUST

. . . God does not ask us not to feel anxious but to trust in Him no matter how we feel.

Thomas Merton

Sure, sure, I hear myself saying: That was easy for Thomas Merton the Trappist, but what about me? I'd rather control and dominate than trust. But then what would I have but me—and is that enough?

ALL BY MYSELF

O God, I'm alone,
It's hard to feel that anyone cares,
Including you, O God.

I wonder if anyone understands
My wanting a friend
Who don't want nothing from me.

Help me to believe
You are my friend
And to know
You are with me.

Keep me from making a fool of myself.

I don't want to become bitter
And filled with hate—
I've seen too much hate

21

I don't want to be angry anymore.

Forgive me, please.
For what I have done,
And help me live right again.

I pray, wondering if you hear me.

Carl Burke

*Yes, I want to be more than myself and I want to
believe that You will be my friend and make me
more. My hate and anger have made me less, and
I want to believe that You can take care of all that
too. But what if I am wrong? But what if right?..*

SELF

**I am more effective when I can listen . . . to myself,
and can be my self.**

Carl Rogers

*But it is so hard to hear. So many voices try to
tell me who I am that I can hardly hear my own
true voice. Do You know who I am? I know You
do, but do I know Your voice?*

JESUS' PRAYER

**According to the evangelists Jesus hardly ever
prayed without sighs and groans, rejoicing or
sadness, fear and tears, loneliness—even shedding
of blood. These emotional outbursts which sparked
and accompanied his prayer were stirred up by
other human beings: his disciples joyfully reporting
their successes, his leave-taking from his friends, his
hope and elation at the prospects of the mission of**

his disciples, his dread of death and separation from his friends. Clearly Jesus was a person who could be affected by others, deeply and emotionally affected. An examination reveals that Jesus' prayer actually presumed an intense immersion in the lives and personalities of the people about him—an involvement that exercised all his human emotions in prayer.

Not only was Jesus' prayer prompted by his friends, but it was on behalf of his friends. Jesus prayed for his close friends, for the poor ones, for the "little ones," for his disciples and future believers as well as for those who persecuted him. His prayer was consistently a prayer for persons. Praying to the person of his Father, he asked that the divine will be accomplished in his own life and mission, and in the lives of his future believers and disciples. His prayers, like his emotions, were people-centered and mission-oriented. The constant object of Jesus' prayer and mission was the needs of others as interpreted by his Father's will to save men: "so that they may be one, just as we are one—so that they may be made perfectly one." (Jn. 17, 23)

How did Jesus acquire this sensitivity and concern for others? He learned it by being with others, living with them, talking with them, listening to them, eating with them. The prayer of Jesus shows clearly that authentic prayer takes place among the People of God in a particular time in history and in a particular culture. Authentic prayer flows from one's willingness to commit himself to finding God's will in his own time and and his own culture. One must be fully in love with and involved in his own world, not some past or imaginary era. Real life, really lived and really responded to: that is the matrix of the prayer of Jesus Christ.

Mathew Fox

This is important: I just can't be thinking of myself and all my turmoils. You prayed for others, Your friends, the poor, even the people who bugged You. You prayed for the world and for Your friends' work in that world. How many opportunities for prayer have I been passing up?

YOU

Wherever men are deaf, you are not there, wherever men are dumb and kill by silence, you are not among them.

Huub Oosterhuis

All that is happening within me without me—and I haven't taken the time to talk with You about it. If I talked more, would I hear more?

CONCERNING JESUS OF NAZARETH

**Jesus, Thou, and I are words—
I know how we are to become deeds too
But I tremble.**

Robert S. Jackson

But am I strong enough to act on what I hear?

THE DAILY NEWS

**I sip my coffee
And skim the news.
Awaiting figures on Niigata earthquake;**

**Again the Minotaur.
Bus hoisted from river, dripping death;
Six tourists lost;
Beyond itinerary.
Fire in turkish bath,
Hot as cremation.
Babies for sale; heavy profit.
Old couples pay most;
Donor keeps virginity.
The Chinese male altered.
Rape at 7E;
Another policeman gone.
Celebrity decides to wed this time.
I peer into familiar brown,
With saucer for horizon,
And I am shown
There is nothing sure beyond the rim.**

Alfeo Marzi

Why do I think that prayer can only come in a dark Church, behind locked doors, or on a retreat? Do You not speak to me in this welter of events I read and see each day? And if I answer, have We not prayed?

DISCOVERY WITHIN US

The way of quiet and grateful joy may also lead to our discovery of the love of God dwelling within us. Someone does us a great kindness, we are freed from a crippling fear or a heavy sorrow, and we feel a surge of deep joy and calm. Behind that change from sorrow to joy, from oppression of heart to freedom, we sense something greater. We read into this joy a reflection of eternal light, and in our gratitude, we know that we have met God and that He has

blessed us. We are filled with a sense of His goodness, His greatness, His sublime mercy. We feel His nearness to us, and the luminous shadow of His blessing, awakening our love.

What we can say about prayer is of little consequence: what matters is what we say in prayer. These words we find for ourselves. They may be shy, weak and poor; they may rise on silver wings to the heavens from a cheerful heart; or they may be drawn with pain from the deep walls of sorrow. They may have in them a resonance like thunder among the hills; or they have in them the softness of summer rain. What matters only is that they come from our heart, and that we desire our hearts to be raised to God with them.

What matters is that the spirit of God lives in our prayer. Such prayer is heard by God. No word of such prayer will be forgotten. For God will give an answer of love to prayers which come to him in words of warm sincerity. That answer will be the giving of Himself to us at every moment of our lives, and most of all in that last hour of decision, when "the shadows lengthen, and the evening comes, and the busy world is hushed, and the fever of life is over, and our work is done. Then in His mercy may He give us a safe lodging and a holy rest, and peace at last!" (Cardinal Newman).

Karl Rahner

Too often I worry if my prayer is good enough, if it is correct. But my prayer has to be the best because it's mine and no other's. That special world within me and no one else gives rise to prayer that You will hear from no one else. And if I don't pray, it seems so strange to say, You will be missing something.

GENUINELY FOR OTHERS

If I am really deeply and genuinely concerned for others and I am going out and taking the needs and seizing the opportunities and I am working to change at least a portion of the world in which I live; If I'm deeply concerned for other people, what's happening, the very redirecting of my consciousness and my affectivity, the very redirecting which is my redemption is actually going on.

Bernard Cooke

So this is what redemption is all about! All that salvation business means looking out for others and working to change the world a little. I wonder if I can do it. . . . Will You help?

LOVE IS DISCOVERY

"Finally, I got you figured."
"I have your number."
"Now I got you pegged."
"I know what you're gonna say
before you open your mouth."
"Ask me a question—I have an answer."
All attitudes that fit THINGS
not people
not love
Not God.
Love is discovery
without end.
When the searching dies
the love dies.
But God,—
"Figure Him out"
"Gather Him inside our walls"
"Understand all about Him."

How easy to say
"I do not understand why this happened to me!
God must not BE."
Job—
remember Job?
He finally got fed up with God.
Things didn't
work out.

God did.

"Friend, where were you
when I founded the earth?
Have you ever entered
the sources of the sea?
Have you ever walked about
behind death's door?

Earnest Larsen

I can't even answer those questions, so how can I
figure You out? I'll just have to keep on discovering.
The world is like a big jigsaw puzzle that You keep
adding pieces to. And guess what, the first pieces
I put together really look different the more I put
around them.

YOU ARE NO STRANGER

✝ How many times, God,
have we been told
that you are no stranger,
remote from those who call upon you
in prayer!
O let us see, God,
and know in our lives now
that those words are true.
Give us faith

and give us the joy
of recognizing your son,
Jesus Christ,
our savior, in our midst.

✝ Make us receptive and open,
and may we accept your kingdom
like children taking bread
from the hands of their father.
Let us live in your peace,
at home with you
all the days of our lives.

✝ Lord God,
your constant love of man
has been handed down
in human words to us.
In this way you are our God and father.
We pray
that we may eagerly listen
to the words of your gospel
and in this way be with you heart and soul
in the fellowship of the Holy Spirit.

Huub Oosterhuis

*That word "open" is so important. I have to be
open to You and Your work because it and You are
all around me. Maybe I don't find You sometimes
because I look in the wrong places.*

COMMUNITY IMPROVISATIONS

What are you most afraid of?

Loneliness.

When was the last time you were lonely?

Yesterday. In my apartment. Nobody was home.

What did you do?

**I washed dishes. I went through my summer
clothes and decided what to keep, listened to music.**

Did you think about being lonely?

**Yes. It was as though I had no connection to
anyone or anything outside the apartment. It was
frightening. I looked out the window facing the
street, the people had no life. I didn't know them.**

From The Bread Is Rising: #4

*Now there is a closed man. He is most peculiarly
closed into his little world. How can he expect to
be anything but lonely if he stays closed inside his
apartment? But I shouldn't be critical, for we are all
locked in lonely apartments—do You have a key?*

THE WORLD IS WOMB

**We who are aware of the need for revolution owe
it to the society we would help to build a kind of
on-going revolution within ourselves, a revolution
which is first of all a revolution of the senses. We
need to work at becoming liberated zones, not just
intellectually nor in certain selected details, but to
release eyes, ears and touch, to permit them whatever voyages they are capable of.**

**Seeing, most fundamentally. Seeing the red-
woods do their thousand-year dance. Seeing the
once virginal place in which a redwood has since
stood but which is now a thousand years vacated.
Seeing the rains and fogs and suns that nourished
the trees, the splintered rocks and fallings which**

were the necessary gifts, the animals and men
that looked and slept, and will look and sleep, in
the branches, hollow places, shadows. The fires
that have survived. Seeing not just what is trapped
by the second hand, but raising the curtain, allowing to be present past and possible, allowing old
bread crusts to give way to a reality feast which is
in communion with more than machines yet notice.
Even seeing the man-eating bear form magically
out of air and water. Seeing that we ourselves have
yet to happen yet have nonetheless been already
absorbed into a community of bread and touch.
Swimming with bears, drinking up water and fish
with great pink tongues, the communion of saints,
corn-planing Indians, blood-stained Marines. Seeing
not as a mirror sees, but seeing so well the world
is healed, time joined, all wedded. Eyes no longer
butcher knives rending the solidarity of existence,
but lovers, doing what lovers do.

    And to hear and touch with the same mir-
aculous catholicity. To discover existence not as a
side-show and zoo but as body and food. Feeling
compelled to reject belief in angels, ironically men
have not yet discovered the reality of rock and
flesh. To be impressed with a glass of water. To say
good morning and really mean it, the words like an
underground brook suddenly reaching the surface.
The gift of seeing, tasting, feeling as another sees,
tastes, feels: to enter into another. To enter into the
hunger of another and to find it our own. To end
the long exile from each other. An end to strangers.
To discover the world is womb.

From The Bread Is Rising: #4

*Yes, I must be open to the life that comes from the
womb-world. I look and listen but I do not see and
hear. Surely You can do better—teach me!*

CONVERSATIONS ON MANY LEVELS

There is a kind of speech below speech which things
carry on with each other as in the psalms, where
we hear day and night passing messages along to
each other (not simply allegory). Speech that is
somehow silence, the poet and the saint can hear
and try to pass along to us. For a long time, poets
have done this with natural things—listened to
them and reported their conversations. Today when
we are surrounded by many man-made wonders
(splendid testimony to carrying out the command
to subdue the earth), the poets and saints move into
this landscape or manscape and listen to a new
kind of conversation and report it. There must be
conversations on many levels—between things and
things, between things and people, between people
and people, between people and God, and, of
course, between things and God. By having a
conversation with things, he made them. The poet
rediscovers how valid or accurate the biblical
account is—not at all un-scientific or anti-scientific
but pre-scientific. It is even now-scientific, a way
science would recognize today. It is a non-abstract
way in which scientists and un-scientists can carry
on their conversation. If conversation means words-
with or with-words, then we can't converse without
people and without things.

    Words are pictures (they have visible forms)
as well as carriers-of-concepts (verbal forms); and
with all of the signs that are around us in our
manscapes and landscapes, there is a great kind of
conversation going on between words and pictures
where one beams on the other, illuminating the
other as persons do to persons.

Corita Kent

How can I talk with You about this wonderful
world-welter of life when there are so many levels
of conversation that I haven't even dreamed of?
The world's been praying and I didn't even know it.

A MONK'S SEARCH

A monastery must always be connected with the
'search for God,' the continual effort to 'realize'
God, to discover the reality of the hidden presence
of God in the depths of the soul. It is the task of the
Christian monk to try to enter into the whole
tradition of Indian sannyasa, **the renunciation of**
the world and all family ties in order to 'realize'
God, to discover the indwelling presence of God in
both nature and the soul. . . . We have to make the
discovery of Christ as Atman, the true Self, of every
being. . . . In Christ we not only discover the
center or ground of our being, but we also find
a meeting point with all other men and with
the whole world of nature. There is a necessary
separation from the world in a monastic life,
a discipline of silence and solitude which is
necessary for the discovery of this inner center
of our being. But this separation should not
divide a monk from the world but on the
contrary enable him to meet the world at the
deepest level of its being.

Dom Bede Griffiths

It's good to be alone with You, for now I can admit
without fear how much I feel lost in the world. The
monk spends his whole life trying to understand
the world at its deepest levels. What chance do I
have who only occasionally scratch below the
surface?

AFFIRMATION

**I don't know who—or what—put the question, I
don't even know when it was put. I don't even
remember answering. But at some moment I did
answer yes to Someone—or Something—and from
that hour I was certain that existence is meaningful
and that, therefore, my life, in self-surrender, had a
goal.**

**From that moment I have known what it
means 'not to look back' and 'to take no thought
for the morrow.'**

Dag Hammarskjold

*But yet I know that You are at the deepest level
and I do have You and that I do have a goal. And
is this not meaning enough for any one man?*

OUR FATHER

Father

**Provider, Responder, source of life
Who answers questions as yet unborn
Whose presence is comfort
Unchanging reality in uncertain motion
Love, measured not, conditionless
—reaching
–supporting
—encouraging
–coaxing
to freedom as sons**

Our Father

**Shared paternity
Circle of humanity
world-wide variety of brothers
Awesome truth
of relationship
so slowly realized
as man draws closer to man
and dawn bows out to the
Fullness of Day**

Who Art in Heaven

**Where? Senseless pondering
His nearness brings heaven
to grime-covered cities
and lowlands
and mountains
and heaven is as far—or as close—
as love touches another**

Hallowed Be Thy Name

Creation bends,
Time extends
    Yahweh IS Father

Thy Kingdom Come

—to proud Publican and unconscious Christian
—to those who wait in hope and to others
    whose frenzied activity
        masks cold despair

Thy Will Be Done on Earth
As It Is in Heaven

To be a listener, a receiver
To be sensitive to echoes of His voice
    from all creation
To interpret the melody of the Composer
. . . "Into thy hands I commend my spirit . . ."
This is crucifixion
    Tomorrow brings new life

Sister Athena

*A vision begins to open up: You as father, the world
as brother, time a stage, and I awakening with new
life and a new role. Will You help me speak my
lines?*

SOMEPLACE

If you insist on poems that rhyme and scan,
    skip this.
What rhymes and scans now?
The world is a big telephone company with big,
    shiny, impressive equipment
Obsolete before it's installed
With overloaded circuits, quick busies and
    operators who
Never hear the first time
And get things mixed up the second
Who think you're concerned if the plug is in
    the hole.
Whether you get to say hello to anybody or not
"One moment, please, for overtime charges."

The world is a big hospital where they have
    to see your Blue Cross card
Before considering your need for a tourniquet
Where doctors practice medicine between
    conferences on investments in
Car washes and pizzarias
And nurses have degrees and domestic troubles
    and coffee but no time
For sick people.
"Visiting hours are over."

The world is a big school with books about
    things that don't matter anymore
And teachers who know a million methods
    for communicating knowledge
They don't have
To students who don't want to learn but insist
    on full certification of
Education so their mommies and daddies
    will stop worrying about their
Getting some place . . . wherever that is.
"You're an underachiever, Francis."

The world is a big church of people who

misbehave in bedrooms
And worry all the time
About people misbehaving in bedrooms
But don't care about misbehavior in stores,
    factories, courts or city hall.
"I've never been so shocked in my life."

The world is a big family
All the members of which dislike each other
And bug each other
While putting down and exploiting each other.
"If you don't like it, you can quit."

The world is a big guy shot on a corner
Lying there with only moments left
Looking through dimming eyes for his mother
    or his girl
And seeing only his blood.
"I told you he'd come to no good end."

The world is a big football team
With great talent at ten positions
A brilliant set of plays and game plan
And a quarterback who always blows it
On third and four.
"I was wide open."

The world is a pair of big lovers
One with a splitting headache and
The other with a runny nose.
"Not tonight, please."

The world is the June Taylor dancers on a
    warped stage
A beautiful girl with the clumsies
A cop with a plugged gun
An Irishman with a German accent
A deaf bartender
An army that wants to go to sea
A guy six four, 230, tough, agile, well trained
    with a great left hook and a Glass jaw

"I followed the directions but it blew up and
    hit Mabel."

It's all going faster and faster and you can't stop
    it or get off
And you might get something done by thinking
    and caring
But who's got time?
"You haven't written and you know how
    I worry."
The hell of it is
God's in the middle of all this.
Someplace.

Bill Jacobs

PRAYER FOR THE MORNING HEADLINES

Mercifully grant peace in our days. Through your
help may we be freed from present distress . . .
Have mercy on women and children homeless in
foul weather, ranting like bees among gutted
barns and stiles. Have mercy on those (like us)
clinging one to another under fire, terror on
terror, grapes the grape shot strikes. Have mercy
on the dead, befouled, trodden like snow in
hedges and thickets. Have mercy, dead man,
whose grandiose gentle hope died on the wing,
whose body stood like a tree between strike
and fall, stood like a cripple on his wooden
crutch. We cry: Halt! we cry: Password! Dishonored
heart, remember and remind, the open sesame:
from there to here, from innocent to us:
Hiroshima, Dresden, Guernica, Selma, Sharpeville,
Coventry, Dachau. Into our history, pass! Seed
hope. Flower peace.

Daniel Berrigan, S.J.

*And the play involves so many people. And You are
there in all of them prompting me. This wide
world of people is my cue, how can I fail?*

TO DISCOVER . . .

that for the first time in human history we have
the means to feed all, we lack only the willingness
to share.

John F. Kennedy

TO DISCOVER . . .

that the ultimate tragedy is not the brutality of
the bad people but the silence of the good people.

Martin Luther King

*And with Your help and the world's, We will speak
and share and show forth a substitute for selfishness
and silence. I am the means, You are the willingness
—together We can.*

FREEDOM

No one can set us free.
For most of our slavery is from within. Like fear.
What we are afraid of prevents, restricts or destroys
   our freedom.
Not that it has the power to do so.
But we surrender to the fears and what we sur-
   render is our freedom. Which is our self.
We can draw lines, build boxes, compose arbitrary
   definitions of our self and never achieve what
   we are free to be beyond the lines, outside the
   boxes, with definitions beyond our imagination to compose.
And we are free to pray, free to stand outside,
   experience the beyond even while the lines are
   still dark, the boxes tight, the definitions rigid.
For freedom is as freedom does.
No one can set us free.
But freedom offered can be taken, accepted,
   appropriated.

Don't let the world around you squeeze you into
its own mold, so that you may prove in practice
that the plan of God for you is good and moves
toward the goal of true maturity.

Romans 12:2

PRAYER FROM A PICKET LINE

Bring the big guardian
angels or devils in black
jackets and white casques
into the act at last. *Love, love at the end.*

The landholders withholding
no more; the jails springing
black and white Easter men;
truncheons like lilies, hoses
gentle as baby pee. *Love, love at the end.*

Bishops down in the ranks
mayors making it too.
Sheriff meek as a shorn lamb
smelling like daisies, drinking dew.
Love, love at the end.

Daniel Berrigan, S.J.

A LITANY FOR THE THIRD WORLD

O God, your son Jesus shared our life and knows what
    it is to be a man,
He made his home in a poor corner of the world and
    must have known hunger from time to time.
He has made himself one with all men everywhere
    and so we can truly say he hungers now
    wherever men do not have enough to eat.
Make us one with him. Help us feed the
    poor of the world.

O God, who starves on the riverbanks of the Ganges,
    who waits numbly by a jungle airfield searching the
      sky for a relief plane,
    who scavenges to find edible scraps in a garbage heap,
Help us see you.

O God, who watches them dump surplus food in oceans,
    who sees food rot for want of a picker,
    who sees crops destroyed to keep prices high,
Open our hearts to the starving.

O God, who works for fifty cents a day picking beets,
    who can't get a job because of his caste,
    who is crippled and can't work and has no food,
Open our eyes to the poor.

O God, the facts cry out:
    In our world 150 million families live in subhuman
    conditions while 30 million live amid prosperity.
    Two-thirds of the world's population doesn't get
    enough to eat each day.
    Thirty million people a year die of starvation,
    more than any war has ever destroyed,
Fill our hearts with outrage.

O God, who can't read, can't write, can't spell,
    can't count, can't hear, can't see, can't speak,
    can't laugh, can't sing, can't stand straight,
    can't sleep, can't play, but only cry and
    feel pain and ache and hide,
Help us see you.

O God, in India one child in five dies in infancy,
    Men live to be only 32,
    83% of the people are illiterate,
Fill our hearts with outrage.

O God, who lives in a favella and sleeps on a dirt floor,
    who lives on a tenth floor tenement alley
    and gets no air,
    who lives in the back of a truck,
Help us to know you.

O God, who can't get a job because
    you're black or yellow,
    who won't be hired again because you once
    complained about working conditions,
    who is replaced by a youth because your hands
    have become gnarled and your back bent,
Help us work for justice.

O God, who is sickened by the hardness of businessmen
    who make necessities unattainable,

who weeps at the sight of children in hospitals
    reeking of contamination,
who is born again in a rice paddy, unattended,
Give us compassion.

O God, the 19 richest nations of the world,
    mostly Christian nations, representing 16 per cent
of the world's people, control 75% of its wealth,
    and half of the world's wealth is spent each
year on weapons for war,
Make the scandal known.

O God, who has sat for hours waiting for an
    overworked doctor to dress a wound,
    who lost a leg because there was no antiseptic
to prevent gangrene,
    who limps because no one ever heard
of corrective surgery,
Help us love you.

O God, who furrows a field with a patched-up plow,
    who raises scraggly vegetables in a field crying for rest,
        who lived on fish until they polluted all the streams,
Help us know your name.

O God, who is present at board meetings
    where important people
        act like they didn't know people need to eat,
who is present at strikes where workers
    are bullied and give in because their
    children are hungry,
who every day sees children with hollow eyes
    and prominent knees between thighbones
    as thin as shinbones,
Help us change this world.

O God, your cries are beginning to be heard from the
    Third World where you live,
    you cry out alienated, angry, yet determined to take
        your place in the world,
    you scream about the inequalities among men
        who should be brothers,
Shatter our indifference.

O God, when you are born again in northeast Brazil

you die half the time,
you rarely live to be over thirty in the
    highlands of Peru,
you have never seen a doctor in Mozambique
    because there is only one for 71,000 people,
Help us know you.

O God, we hear you shouting revolution in the streets of
    Montevideo,
    we see you taking to the hills to fight a
        corrupt dictator,
    we hold your dying hand, once again a victim
        of tribal warfare,
Help us understand your plight.

O God, who asks only for a small plot of land
    to grow food,
    who asks only the freedom to live without fear
        and oppression,
    who asks only for the right to have some say
        about those who rule you,
Shatter our distance from you.

O God, we find men who call themselves Christians
    opposing change and defending with force
a corrupt social order,
    we find churchmen who live casually with
injustice and rant "Communist"! whenever anyone
    suggests a better distribution of wealth,
    yet we find men of no faith ready to sacrifice
        themselves for your children.
Make us truly Christian.

O God, the scandal is no longer hidden,
    it is out in the open now,
no man with conscience can ignore the
    situation any longer.
The poor have seen our affluence, our luxury,
    our tanks and guns,
Make us one with them.
Help us build a new world.

James Young, C.S.P.

Sometimes I get that tight-up-tight feeling and just want to be free of all people and all cares and worries. But is that freedom—or is it flight? What will I do? What lines, what boxes, what definitions hem my self in? I know I can be more, but where?

CHRISTIANITY AND COMMUNITY

For us, to say Christian means to say: community, new life, co-existence, peace, sharing. As Bonhoeffer has written: "There is in fact only one religion from which the concept of community is inseparable, and that is Christianity." The Church is disfunctional in its purpose so long as it conceives itself as a "religious organization" (or a religion for that matter). Its "religious" life is, or should be, indeed, a secular life, demanding an orientation toward the transformation of man.

The Church is this:

It is about people, about humanity renewed, reborn to freedom and love, through water and the Spirit.

The Church is meant to be a sign, a beginning of the renewed human community, pointing to the world's true being. The Christian life is meant to be a breakthrough of Christ's way of unity and shalom into the old world of division and hostility. (Eph 4: 1-16)

This new life is not lived in a churchly institution isolated from reality and the life of the world. We are a segment of the world; and if there is momentary separation or disengagement it is to prepare for engagement, not to become apolitical or ahuman. We are a "serving segment." As Dietrich Bonhoeffer wrote: "The Church is her true self only when she exists for humanity." Finally, the Church is a liberation movement, a process of being liberated from every conceivable form of establishment/status quo.

It is almost embarrassing to some Christians to mention the name of Jesus. Christian terms explode all sorts of bad images and hang-ups within us. Because we do not want to be placed in a "churchy" bag, we dismiss the riches of Christian tradition. It is ironic to see Christians who can quote Chairman Mao but cannot quote Jesus of Nazareth. It is ironic to see New Left students, not Christians, saying: you can be in, but not always of the world. It is ironic to see some hippies, not Christians, separate themselves from a system and hierarchy of values which they consider corrupt. It is refreshing to meet young men and women, who would not accept the label of Christian, yet who can speak freely of Jesus, truth, community, communication, peace, justice. It is ironic to see a poster on an S.D.S. wall appreciative of the life of Jesus: WANTED: JESUS CHRIST . . . warning: this man is dangerous and is challenging the American way of life.

David Kirk

Sharing . . . serving segment . . . liberation movement . . . New Left. . . . Who is a Christian? A Christian should be concerned about people, about a renewed humanity, about freedom and love. Am I a Christian? I wonder—and what happened to vigil lights anyway?

I SEE WHITE AND BLACK, LORD

I see white teeth in a black face.
I see black eyes in a white face.
Help us to see persons, Jesus—not a black person
or a white person, a red person, but human persons.

Malcolm Boyd

*What's the difference between seeing a face and
seeing a person? It must have something to do
with loving. You can't love a face. It must have
something to do with community. You can't have a
community of faces.*

BUDDHISM

Unless we agree to suffer we cannot be free from
suffering.

*You can't suffer if you really want to do something
I wonder if I really give a damn about anybody
else? You just have to say you're for love and
community and civil rights and equal opportunity
and all that. But do I really want to do something
for someone else—something that he wants and I
may not want?*

LETTER FROM THE BIRMINGHAM CITY JAIL

. . . There was a time when the Church was very
powerful. It was during that period when the
early Christians rejoiced when they were deemed
worthy to suffer for what they believed. In those
days the Church was not merely a thermometer
that recorded the ideas and principles of popular
opinion; it was a thermostat that transformed the
mores of society. Wherever the early Christians
entered a town the power structure got disturbed
and immediately sought to convict them for being
"disturbers of the peace" and "outside agitators."
But they went on with the conviction that they
were a "colony of heaven" and had to obey God
rather than man. They were small in number but
big in commitment. They were too God-intoxicated
to be "astronomically intimidated." They brought
an end to such ancient evils as infanticide and
gladiatorial contest.

Things are different now. The contemporary
Church is so often a weak, ineffectual voice with
an uncertain sound. It is so often the arch-supporter
of the status quo. Far from being disturbed by
the presence of the Church, the power structure
of the average community is consoled by the
Church's silent and often vocal sanction of things
as they are.

But the judgment of God is upon the Church
as never before. If the Church of today does not
recapture the sacrificial spirit of the early Church,
it will lose its authentic ring, forfeit the loyalty of
millions, and be dismissed as an irrelevant social
club with no meaning for the twentieth century.
I am meeting young people every day whose
disappointment with the Church has risen to
outright disgust.

Maybe again I have been too optimistic. Is
organized religion too inextricably bound to the
status quo to save our nation and the world?

Maybe I must turn my faith to the inner spiritual Church, the church within the Church, as the true ecclesia and the hope of the world. But again I am thankful to God that some noble souls from the ranks of organized religion have broken loose from the paralyzing chains of conformity and joined us as active partners in the struggle for freedom. They have left their secure congregations and walked the streets of Albany, Georgia, with us. They have gone through the highways of the South on torturous rides for freedom. Yes, they have gone to jail with us. Some have been kicked out of their churches and lost the support of their Bishops and fellow ministers. But they have gone with the faith that right defeated is stronger than evil triumphant. These men have been the leaven in the lump of the race. Their witness has been the spiritual salt that has preserved the true meaning of the Gospel in these troubled times. They have carved a tunnel of hope through the dark mountain of disappointment.

I hope the Church as a whole will meet the challenge of this decisive hour. But even if the Church does not come to the aid of justice, I have no despair about the future. I have no fear about the outcome of our struggle in Birmingham, even if our motives are presently misunderstood. We will reach the goal of freedom in Birmingham and all over the nation, because the goal of America is freedom. Abused and scorned though we may be, our destiny is tied up with the destiny of America. Before the pilgrims landed at Plymouth, we were here. Before the pen of Jefferson etched across the pages of history the majestic words of the Declaration of Independence, we were here. For more than two centuries our fore-parents labored in this country without wages; they made cotton "king"; and they built the homes of their masters in the midst of brutal injustice and shameful humiliation—and yet out of a bottomless

vitality they continued to thrive and develop. If the inexpressible cruelties of slavery could not stop us, the opposition we now face will surely fail. We will win our freedom because the sacred heritage of our nation and the eternal will of God are embodied in our echoing demands. . . .

Martin Luther King Jr.

And I can hear You starting to ask, to call me past lines, out of boxes, across definitions. Martin King speaks but I hear You. He could criticize the Church, You always will—but I am the Church, I act like the Church that he criticizes, I must be silent in shame. Have I the nerve, the faith, to be part of the church within the Church? I would like to be like Martin, but he was killed and I'm no hero. Do You think I could be just a little heroic?

MY LEGS WERE PRAYING

"When I marched with Martin Luther King in Selma," says Rabbi Hechel, "I felt my legs were praying." Heschel prays in words as well as deeds. "If I thought God were just an impersonal ocean, I couldn't pray either way. An I, after all, cannot pray to an it."

Time

Amen! If I were walking with black men in Selma, Alabama, each step would be shouting: I'm here to help these people and I know You want me to keep on walking and helping.

DOING

Man recovers his humanity by doing **the truth.**

Ivan Illich

I wonder if I would have been more of a man if I had been with Martin King and Rabbi Heschel or at least wanted to?

TRANSFORMING THE PROFANE

One of the great things that is happening in the Church today is—we're beginning to find out that maybe what we call secular is also part of the sacred, and that the only way to get anything sacred short of God is to transform the profane.

At the foundation, therefore, of any theology of involvement, there must be an understanding of the Incarnation and its implications. What this

means for our own spirituality, for the attitude we should have in going out into an apostolic situation, is that we must have a great respect for creation and, within creation, a particular reverence for man. Christ reflects such an attitude and, in doing so, fulfills the revelation of the Old Testament, which insists that when God created, he created all things good. Nothing that God created was evil and there is no other God who, somewhere else, created evil things. There is one God and his creation is good. Evil came, not from God, but from man's abuse of his freedom, his unwillingness to accept the fact that he is man and not God.

In approaching the things God has made, one must see them as good; "secular" and "profane" should not be two words that are used to denigrate reality. We talk constantly about the danger of "secularism." There is no doubt a certain danger of this kind, but I believe one of the great things happening in the Church today is that we are beginning to find that the secular is also part of the sacred; that the only way to reach the sacred, short of God, is to transform the profane. The sacred is not something existing in the abstract. Grace is the transformation of men, and there can be no grace in existence unless there are men.

Bernard Cooke

I feel a definition about to dissolve! Working for civil rights a Christian thing? But if that's not transforming the profane by respecting man, what is? But if civil rights is Christian, then. . . . But don't You rush me, I want to be free but maybe not too free too fast.

WE LIVE IN WONDER

God does not die on the day when we cease to believe in a personal deity, but we die on the day when our lives cease to be illumined by the steady radiance, renewed daily, of a wonder, the source of which is beyond all reason.

Dag Hammarskjold

Could it be that all this "God is dead" talk is just an admission by us that we have stopped trying to live and transform the life around us? Maybe I don't want a live God—You might ask too much.

EARTHBOUND MAN

Only earthbound man still clings to the dark and poisoning superstition that his world is bounded by the nearest hill, his universe ended at river shore, his common humanity enclosed in the tight circle of those who share his town and views and the color of his skin.

Robert F. Kennedy

Yet all You want is to open me up to the fullness of the life all around me. You want me to dream dreams and see visions and act courageously to make them real. What else is freedom for?

WHO AM I?

Who am I? They often tell me
I stepped from my cell's confinement
calmly, cheerfully, firmly,
like a Squire from his country house.

Who am I? They often tell me
I used to speak to my wardens
freely and friendly and clearly,
as though it were mine to command.

Who am I? They also tell me
I bore the days of misfortune
equably, smilingly, proudly,
like one accustomed to win.

Am I then really that which other men tell of?
Or am I only what I myself know of myself?
Restless and longing and sick, like a bird in a cage,
struggling for breath, as though hands were com-
        pressing my throat,
yearning for colours, for flowers, for the voices of
        birds,
thirsting for words of kindness, for neighbourliness,
tossing in expectation of great events,
powerlessly trembling for friends at an infinite
        distance,
weary and empty at praying, at thinking, at
        making,
faint, and ready to say farewell to it all.

Who am I? This or the Other?
Am I one person to-day and to-morrow another?
Am I both at once? A hypocrite before others,
and before myself a contemptible woebegone
        weakling?
Or is something within me still like a beaten
        army
fleeing in disorder from victory already achieved?

Who am I? They mock me, these lonely questions
   of mine.
Whoever I am, Thou knowest, O God, I am
thine!

Dietrich Bonhoeffer

*Look at Dietrich Bonhoeffer. He did great things
with his freedom, but even he was afraid of it and
was tempted to doubt what he could be. Maybe a
weak man can be a great man too? Well, whatever
and whoever I am, I am Yours too! And I want to
be free for You.*

SAYING YES

Michael Novak, who spent thirteen years in
Catholic seminaries, is not concerned that such
student meditation does not often focus on God.
"Prayer does not depend upon our conception of
God," he believes, "because our conception may be
the true God or a figment of our own imagination."
After all, he goes on, the test most great Christian
mystics set for themselves was how well they lived
with others after their ecstatic transports were
over. "The essence of prayer," he concludes, "is a
yes to God and His World. And its basic form is
Mary's response to the Angel Gabriel: 'Be it done
unto me according to Thy word'."

Time

*Such a simple little word, a "yes"—but by saying it
I can be so much more, I can be all things. Yes! so
be it!*

TIME TO CREATE

A few seminaries are beginning to try to bridge the
language gap. The most notable experiment is at
New York's Jewish Theological Seminary where
Rabbi Avraham Holtz teaches his students to
approach prayer through analysis of old Hebrew
forms and themes, then encourages them to look
at modern poetry and compose prayers of their
own. "I want my students to realize that now is the
time for us to create," Holtz explains. "Obviously,
if prayer is to be significant, it has to give
expression to aspects of our real life."

Time

*Why do I look up when I want to pray? I should
look around me. I start to use words—"vouchsafe
. . . deign . . . grace . . . salvation . . . eternal"—but
those words don't really say it. Maybe some of
these do: "riot . . . Vietnam . . . help."*

CONTEMPLATION

"We haven't emphasized enough the role of
contemplation in the Christian life," complains Dr.
Michael Ramsey, "so people are finding it in
non-Christian movements."

Time

*It seems that it's people like Mia Farrow, the
Beatles, and Sybil Burton who make the news for
praying. Maybe we Christians have been missing
something—maybe I have been missing something!*

PROLOGUE OF SAINT JOHN

In the beginning the Word already was;
the Word was at home with God;
Yet God he was, the Word!
He was in the beginning present with God.

All through him came into being;
apart from him not one thing came to be.
What was made found life in him,
and this life was the light of men.
That light shines in the darkness,
for the darkness has never put it out.

He was the genuine light
that illumines every man;
he was making his appearance in the world.
He was present in the world—
the world was made by him—
yet the world did not recognize him.

To his own land he came;
still his own folk did not accept him.
But to those who did accept him—
to those who believe in his name—
he gave power to become God's children:
those who were begotten
not by blood,
nor by desire of the flesh,
nor by the desire of any man,
but by God.

Thus, the Word became flesh,
and pitched his tent among us.
And we have beheld his glory—
glory from his Father as only Son:
the essence of God's mercy and fidelity . . .
Yes, of his abundance we have all received our
    share.

grace instead of grace!
The Law was a gift through Moses:
this mercy, this fidelity came into being through
    Jesus Christ.
God no man has ever seen:
His only Son, who shares the secrets of his
    Father's heart,
has personally acted as our interpreter.

Translation By David Stanley, S.J.

Do I fear to pray because it looks like a cop-out, a flight into fancy away from the facts! But that's not what prayer and religion are all about, or so it seems John and Christ are saying. Christ is our leader and if He as God's Son had to come into this world and give it light, how can I as God's son do anything but get involved with this world and give it some more light? Does not following Christ mean following Him into the world and flesh?

A PRAYER
FOR MAKING THE RIGHT CHOICES

God, please help us from doing stupid things. Why don't you make us stand up for the right thing? When you ain't got no place to play a ball game, or tag, it's easy to get into a mess even if you didn't want to. Hope you will remember that. When you don't have many friends and you are trying to get one it's easy to do what he wants you to. Hope you'll remember that, too. So help us, please, to do the right thing and we will be thankful to you.

Carl Burke

Bringing light means doing right. Now that's easy to talk about but when it comes time for doing. . .? But there is much to do and it's so important, I'll just have to try and You'll just have to help.

PRAYER IS . . .

Prayer is a constant struggle to change ourselves. It is a battle to realize ever more fully that God has loved us, and loves us still. Clearly, then, prayer is more a process of man being changed than of man calling to God to change or to effect change elsewhere. By sending his Son, not only historically, but personally in each stage and person in history, God is already effecting change. God's total commitment to the salvation of man and his world is the medium, the field, the fundamental reality of prayer. Without it there is no prayer; with it there are no limits to the depth and scope of the relationship possible between man and God—no limits, that is, other than man's willingness to be changed and accept being changed.

The real problem in prayer is not that God is effecting no changes in the world; nor that he is distant; nor even that he is silent. The problem is that, being so close and so broadly diffused, men still miss him. That is why the process of prayer is the process of man changing, not God. One travels a route often marked by desperation, and many speak of death and misery and the absence of God. But the reality, known by faith, is quite the contrary.

Mathew Fox

How can I be timid? You and Christ say: Be all you can. Why do I hesitate?

A PRAYER

Lord,
I am confused. There are so many of us here.
What do we do? Where do we begin?
How do we really love each other?
    each show-off
    each loner
    each person who grates us
        uses us
        rejects us?
How do we really know one another
    help one another
    rid one another of superficial human respect
        face-value judgements
        meaningless talk?
Lord
There are so many of us here
    so many who wander through
        push through
        run through
    so many who are bitter
        sightless
        afraid.
Yes, Lord
I am grateful for those here who inspire us
    strengthen us
    those with the courage to lead us
        to challenge us
        to be themselves with us

But, Lord
What about the rest of us?
If we are strangers to one another now
   will we be brother to your people later on?
If we don't give ourselves now
   will we offer ourselves later on?

Lord,
I am confused. There are so many of us here.
Where do we begin? What do we do?
We do not know now but we are eager to change
　　　　help us to change.
Lord,
　　　help us to stop talking
　　　　　to start listening
　　　　　to start believing.

Dennis M. Corrado

Yet I'm certain, too, that somehow under all the
confusion I can make it. Maybe I fall short because
I talk too much and don't listen for You enough.
You speak to me in all the events of my life, hinting,
coaxing, coaching, and even pushing me forward.
Am I afraid to listen?

APOSTLES' CREED

I believe in God, the Father, the Almighty,
creator of heaven and earth.

I believe in Jesus Christ, his only Son, our Lord.

He was conceived by the power of the Holy
Spirit and born of the Virgin Mary.

He suffered under Pontius Pilate,
was crucified, died, and was buried.

He went down to the dead.

On the third day he rose again.

He ascended into heaven,
and is seated at the right hand of God,
the Father, the Almighty.

He will come again to judge the living and
the dead.

I believe in the Holy Spirit,
the holy catholic Church,
the communion of saints,
the forgiveness of sins,
the resurrection of the body,
and the life eternal. Amen.

Officially Proposed
Ecumenical Version

*It's very simple to read, but it could be so rich if
I could live it. After all, why would You let Christ
leave if You didn't want us to carry on His work?
It's up to me.*

WHO WANTS TO LISTEN?

Saint Paul exclaims,
"God's word is a living thing!"
Living—
that means
it's actual,
being spoken at this very moment,
continually and tirelessly repeated,
born again in God's heart every day
to be transmitted to living men,
and it's always fresh,
new for each and every man,
personal,
meant to illuminate him individually.
This word's "the true light that enlightens everyone
who comes into the world."
There's not a soul on earth God doesn't speak to.

The keenest suffering and the bitterest complaint
of modern unbelievers
arise from the "silence of God,"
against which they seem to bang their head
whenever they try, in all sincerity, to look for Him.
"After all," replies the doctor in Camus' La Peste,
"since the order of the world is dominated by death
perhaps it's better for God that we don't believe in
Him
but war against death for all we're worth,
without looking up to heaven,
where He sits perfectly silent."
What answer do we have to this despair?
Are we convinced He's spoken to us?
Do we believe wholeheartedly in His living word,
in that ever-present voice
which keeps uttering,
for each of us,
the words that can heal?
"Say but the word . . ."

Our faith in God's word is measured by our faith
in His love.
We don't really believe He speaks to us
because we don't really believe He loves us.
What's a saint?
It's someone who believes that God loves him.
"We've come to know and believe in God's love
for us."
Anyone who believes God loves him
knows that God speaks to him.

God hasn't ceased being Revelation
any more than He's ceased being Love.
He enjoys expressing Himself.
Since He's Love,
He must give Himself,

**share His secrets,
communicate with us
and reveal Himself to anyone
who wants to listen.**

Louis Evely

*Maybe I do listen but not enough or in the right
places? Sure, I listen at Mass and in church; but
why do I stop there? Your word is meant to be my
light—doesn't that mean that You may speak to me
at any time that I may be ready to listen? Keep
talking, I'm adjusting the sound.*

SLOW DOWN . . . COOL IT

**Make us slow down and cool it but good, God
So we can get with it.
We need to find out where we is going
To find out how to be happy
And do good things.
We want to be a good guy and in a way we don't.
Mostly 'cause we don't see any point in it.
What's it going to get us is what we ask you.
What's the use if you still live in a dump
And all that happens is you get beat up?
These is the things we ask you.**

Carl Burke

*It's time to be honest—I've been letting the good
side of me do all the talking. Maybe I'm blind or
maybe I'm scared, but sometimes I just don't do
the good things I should. I wonder why . . .?*

REDISCOVERY

In part, this rediscovery is a reaction against the secular life-style of the modern Christian West. "The disease of affluence is not only an obesity of body," observes Quaker philosopher Douglas Steere, "but also obesity of soul. Students are appalled at the self-absorption of the West in its own never-ending spiral of production and accumulation of wealth."

Time

Am I fat in my soul? Does my desire for money and all the things that I can get with it get in the way of Your voice?

LIFE

I am the resurrection and the life. He who believes in me, though he be dead, shall live. And he who lives and believes in me shall never die.

Gospel of St. John

All the things that make up the "good life"—cars, clothes, capers—don't keep me from dying. In fact they don't necessarily make "life" all that "good." There is more to it than that—and You offer that more.

TOUCHING BEING TOUCHED

"I don't know how to talk to you," I said. I had talked too much and listened too little. It was then that I realized with a sense of desperation and near panic that I could not wrench off my mask and confront this girl face to face. I was lost, unable to hear myself in my voice. Very dimly, then, I began to see what has become blazingly clear today: students must help their teachers, must keep them in touch with what is human in themselves, keep them from losing the faces they saw in the mirror when they were young—just as teachers must help students realize and refine their own resources and motivate them to reshape the world in their own image. If the students fail to reclaim and sustain their teachers, the teachers will fail to liberate their students, and the cycle of depersonalization will be perpetuated.

The girl kept apologizing for bothering me, in a tone of voice that said, "It is too bad you are so inhuman." She was impertinent, and I was annoyed, but I was also grateful. She did not realize that there comes a time when you discover that your parents cannot understand you and that they require your understanding. But she helped me to perceive that I was becoming a machine with a facelike mask, and that it was time to revolt and reform. I was a success. That was the trouble.

In graduate school I had learned to subordinate all human impulses into a disciplined drive to produce, to produce first a Ph.D., and then articles, and then books. What Herbert Marcuse, in Eros and Civilization, terms "the performance principle": that is reality in the university, as well as in our entire society. Production is the only thing that matters. Everything is a means toward that end. Production, promotion, prestige–this is our trinitarian God.

Motive

I and my successful colleagues have become streamlined projectiles—dead and deathdealing because we have forgotten that people are not means. Students and teachers cannot meet face to face until we realize that it is not the structure of our universities alone, but our sense of reality, our value system that are freezing faces into masks. We will not have time for students until we have time for ourselves.

The most horrifying aspect of my experience with this one student did not appear until about a week after our encounter in my home. First she wrote a very powerful essay on Camus and "the absurd," saying that in my home she had realized the meaning of isolation and absurdity. Then we had another talk. It was a genuine conversation, but I was stunned to discover that she decided that she had been romanticizing herself, that I was right; people do not have time for one another. That is the way things are. Alienation is inevitable. Now I tried to persuade her and myself that this was just sane-sounding insanity. We must not resign ourselves to a situation that can be transformed. But (and this seems to me to be very significant) my conversation with this girl will not resume in the fall because she has transferred to another university—not because of our relationship, I hasten to add. Students are almost as mobile as professors. Faces disappear.

Motive

But I'm leaping ahead again. I want to reach out and touch You and the meaning of the entire universe, but I overlook the guy who's in trouble. I want to be open with You, yet I close myself off from all others. Can't I see the connection?

THE ONE USED CAR THAT WAS SNITCHED

There was a used-car lot at the corner of Main and Fillmore. The owner had one hundred heaps on it. If one of the heaps was snitched would the owner go and look for it? You bet he would. He would never give up looking till he found it.

Suppose he found it at North and Main. What would he do? Well, he would "rev it up, man" to see if it's OK. When he gets it back to the yard he would show it to the gang to have it checked out. If it checks out OK they would all be happy, 'cause that one heap is just as important as the 99 that no one stole. Well, this is the way it will be when one guy goes straight. One guy is just as important to God as 99 are who have always been OK. This is for real—God is just as interested in you as the used-car lot owner is in his heap.

Carl Burke

Not only are you interested in me but in each man. Am I?

PENANCE

Help me, O God, since
I do not understand my own actions,
For I do not do what I want,
but I do the very thing I hate.

I can will what is right,
but I cannot do it.
For I do not do the good I want.

Romans 7:15

I know I will fail to be all that I can, but should that stop me from trying?

TRUST

God does not ask you not to feel anxious, but to trust in Him no matter how you feel.

Thomas Merton

Will I?. .

THE REALITY IS CHRIST

I am the real shepherd
I am the door
I am the living bread which came down from
    heaven
I am the resurrection and the life
I am the true vine
I am the Alpha and the Omega
I am the first and the last, and the living one;
I am the way, the truth, the life.

If any one is thirsty let him come to me and drink.
Whoever drinks of this water will thirst again, but
    whoever drinks of the water that I shall give
    him will never thirst; the water that I shall
    give him will become in him a spring of water
    welling up to eternal life.
I and the Father are one.

The Way

Amen. So be it. Let me drink deep of this life.
Teach me, Christ.

LOVE

Love.
Yesterday the TV announcer applied it to a hair
spray. Or was it a car? Mouth wash?

And last Saturday a boy and a girl tried to talk of
it and their words ran sudsy in their mouths because
their dialogue seemed to them like patches from a
soap-opera. Or was it the late show?

Some bebuttoned types announced they were for
it. As though you could achieve it by pinning it
to your lapel.

And a young couple found peace in the struggle to
realize it.

A young girl prayed that it would happen to her.

And someone else prayed because it had.
Which isn't unusual.
Because the buttons are also prayers. Arent' they?
Sort of?

I am the Good Shepherd and I know those that are
mine and my sheep know me, just as the Father
knows me and I know the Father. And I am giving
my life for the sake of my sheep.

John, 12:14-16

A PARABLE

Once upon a time there was a young girl, an orphan, who grew up in coarse surroundings. Her foster parents were hard and rough, and had never wanted her. Never as a baby or as a growing child had she known the subtle intimacy of a true home. She had never been loved.

And then she grew into a young woman. Daily encounter with disparagement, egotism and brutality hardened her heart. All she knew was self-defense, daily surly bickering to make sure of a minimum of security and right. To the best of her knowledge, it had always been so in the past, and it would remain so in the future: biting in order not to be bitten—the law of the jungle. She had no faith in man; she had not even faith in herself.

Her whole appearance betrayed the solitude in which the soul of her youth was living. She toiled and moiled, dressed in cheap, graceless attire. Her one means of escape from hopeless emptiness was rough and rowdy amusement. Selfish, suspicious and uncouth, with bitterness distorting her mouth, she was aware that she had no beauty and that what men wanted was her body for a few lustful moments.

There lived in the same city a young man, hale and strong. His sunny youth, spent in the midst of loving parents, brothers and sisters, shone in his gaze and sang in his voice. His step and speech were assured and firm, as is the case with those who have found peace. He was a good man.

One bright morning in spring, the miracle happened. The young man met the girl by chance. Moved in his innermost self, his heart went out to her. With the eyes of love, he saw right through and beyond her shabby vulgarity. He looked out for her; he spoke to her with the simplicity of a conquered heart. But she laughed in his face at first, addressed him in crude, unmannered language. She thought he was ridiculous.

But tact, patience and respect found their way at last to a remnant of yearning which lay still unwithered in the depth of the girl's being. For the first time in her life, she was appreciated for her own sake—the greatest need of human nature. Yet the beauty he discovered in her came not from her but from his love.

Love has been a creative power since the beginning of the world. The young man's deference and appreciation stirred up in her a nascent self-reliance, a foretaste of peace and quiet, of inner self-assurance. And timidly, gropingly, the young woman awakened to first love. She shyly began taking care of her appearance, though gaudily still and without elegance. His tenderness and his example refined her taste. Beauty came to her with the first smile.

Soon they became absorbed in each other. They steadily drew together in a selfless exchange of pure mutual love. What had happened really? Or better: what had come into being? That girl had been granted a great favor, a matchless present, a gift she did not deserve: the favor of love.

After the long, barren winter of her youth, a seed had been sown in her innermost self; it was ready to spring into life. Though still very much herself, she was already another person. She experienced a soothing security, welling up from unsuspected regions within her; she grew steadily in strength and depth, in proportion as her formerly cherished convictions were pulled up by the roots. It was like a painful dying. All the distrust, hatred and vindictiveness she had so far nursed in herself, whatever she had clung to with the despair of a drowning person, she had now to let go; she had to resign herself to the sensation of being stripped bare, bereaved of all. A harrowing agony, indeed, but one of which life is born.

Like a ship tossed on the waves and driven from her course, the girl tried another tack. She steered to the unknown: she made the leap of faith in another. The aggressive self-assertiveness, the armor in which she had shielded herself so far, was torn off her. She attempted the leap of hope in another who would in the future stand surety for her. Meanwhile, an unsuspected marvel happened: she felt enriched by her new state of bereavement, secure and anchored in her surrender. Faith and hope ripened into real love, the final leap, indispensable to anyone who wants both to lose himself and to find himself in another. The girl had lost everything she had, but what she lost she recovered superabundantly. She ceased putting her trust in appearances and now saw more deeply into things. She discovered the beauty of her surrounding world—the setting sun, the violet in the shade, the light in the eyes of a child, the laughter in a voice. She saw everything through the eyes of her beloved. She became another being altogether; for the first time, she was her true self. Her injured youth lived on in her, but it now began to develop along the lines of generosity and disinterested care of others–in a wealth of gratitude.

A beautiful tale, indeed. The one thing in it which leaves us somewhat skeptical is whether there ever was a young man powerful enough to work such a miracle. We read of the custom in honor among the conquistadores that when they were caught in a storm at sea, they vowed marriage with the first penniless girl God would put on their path after a safe return home, with the provisio, naturally, that the girl be sound of limb and morals. Whatever view one takes of the parable or of the conquistadores' custom, it is sure that only a very pure and powerful love can change bitterness and hatred into a return of love. No mere man, however, can achieve even that much,

for wickedness is rooted more deeply in our nature than we dare suspect. That is why there had to appear a Man without sin, a Man possessing God's own heart. And when He came, the tale became reality.

Peter Fransen

Love is a little word that has the whole world largely disturbed. So important—everybody says so—and so elusive—for me at least. Christ said it was His message: how can I be a Christian if I don't know what love is? But there seems to be some lesson about love in this parable. First lesson: love is for people. Second lesson: love is wonderful because it produces wonderful things in me and in others. Third lesson: love, born of faith and hope, gives new vision. Do I really believe that Christ can and does love me and that wonders and new vision await my response to that love? How do I respond?

A CONTEMPLATION

Note. **Two preliminary observations:**

(1) **Love should be expressed in doing rather than in protesting.**

(2) **Love consists in a reciprocal interchange, the lover handing over and sharing with the beloved his possessions, gifts and capacities, and** *vice versa.* **So, if one of them has learning, he gives it to the other who lacks it; so too, with positions of honor or material possessions; and the other does the same.**

The usual preparatory prayer.

First preliminary. **The picture. I am standing in the presence of our Lord God, His angels and His saints, who are pleading for me.**

Second preliminary. **Asking for what I want. Here it will be to beg for a deep-felt appreciation of all the blessings I have been given, that out of the fullness of my gratitude I may become completely devoted to His Divine Majesty in effective love.**

First heading. **Recall the good things I have had from creation: my redemption, personal gifts. I will rouse myself to reckon how much our Lord God has done for me, how much that is His own He has shared with me; I will further consider the divine plan whereby this same Lord wants to give me all that it is in His power to give.**

I then turn to myself and try to see what reason and justice demand that I offer, nay, give, His Divine Majesty in return—all that belongs to me, and with it all that I am in myself—in the spirit of one who makes a present out of a great love:

Take, Lord, into Your possession, my complete freedom of action, my memory, my understanding and my entire will, all that I have, all that I own: it is Your gift to me, I now return it to You. It is all Yours, to be used simply as You wish. Give Your Love and Your grace; it is all I need.

Second heading. **See God living in His creatures:**
in matter, giving it existence,
in plants, giving them life,
in animals, giving them consciousness,
in men, giving them intelligence.
So He lives in me, giving me existence, life, consciousness, intelligence.
More, He makes me His temple, since I have been created wearing the image and likeness of God.
Again I will turn to myself, as indicated under the first heading, or in some other way that I prefer.
(This also applies to the following headings.)

Third heading. **Think of God energizing,** as though He were actually at work, in every created reality, in the sky, in matter, plants and fruits, herds and the like: it is He who creates them and keeps them in being, He who confers life or consciousness, and so on.
Then I turn to myself.

Fourth heading. **Realize that all gifts and benefits come from above.** My moderate ability comes from the supreme Omnipotence on high, as do my sense of justice, kindliness, charity, mercy, and so on, like sunbeams from the sun or streams from their source.
I will end, as was said above, by turning to myself.
In conclusion, a colloquy and an *Our Father.*

St. Ignatius of Loyola

My response is becoming clear: doing and sharing, not talking and keeping, that's a start for love. And I see a field for love: the world, where I stand in the middle, between God and my brothers, with love binding us all together.

I WAS LONELY

'When the Son of Man comes in his glory,
escorted by all the angels, then he will take his
seat on his throne of glory. All the nations
will be assembled before him and he will
separate men one from another as the shepherd
separates sheep from goats. He will place the
sheep on his right hand and the goats on his left.
Then the King will say to those on his right hand,
"Come, you whom my Father has blessed,
take for your heritage the kingdom prepared
for you since the foundation of the world. For
I was hungry and you gave me food; I was
thirsty and you gave me drink; I was a stranger
and you made me welcome; naked and you
clothed me, sick and you visited me, in prison
and you came to see me." Then the virtuous will
say to him in reply, "Lord, when did we see
you hungry and feed you; or thirsty and give you
drink? When did we see you a stranger and make
you welcome; naked and clothe you; sick or in
prison and go to see you?" And the King will
answer, "I tell you solemnly, in so far as
you did this to one of the least of these brothers
of mine, you did it to me." Next he will say to
those on his left hand, "Go away from me, with
your curse upon you to the eternal fire prepared
for the devil and his angels. For I was hungry
and you never gave me food; I was thirsty and
you never gave me anything to drink; I was a
stranger and you never made me welcome,
naked and you never clothed me, sick and in
prison and you never visited me." Then it will be
their turn to ask, "Lord, when did we see you
hungry or thirsty, a stranger or naked, sick or in
prison, and did not come to your help?"
Then he will answer, "I tell you solemnly, in so
far as you neglected to do this to one of the
least of these, you neglected to do it to me."
And they will go away to eternal punishment,
and the virtuous to eternal life.'

The Jerusalem Bible

EVEN MISSISSIPPI

This still young world of ours
is taking on the ancient look
of starvation-dead babies.
Famine has become the only
affirmation for too many,
food the only meaning;
there are mouths eating
in too many dreams,
in too few homes.
Waste is at work in bodies.
Withering is a world-wide pastime.
Hunger is a lengthening shadow
arching from China, over India,
cutting through holy lands
to European cities and valleys
of, even, Mississippi USA.
Two of us out of three
stand with empty hands,
palms turned please and up.
They go sadly, with faces
long and desperate for their children.
They quaver for a crumb.

II
We are judged by hunger now,
we who adorn ourselves, doing well,
who feed more by far
to our dogs and precious cats
than to those shadowed men
whose bones are numbered,
whose sides are pierced
by what we throw away.
God, help us who have this dreaded
power to feed every of your sons.

Help us in our affluence
to, in fact, begin to do so.
And, God, help those especially
whose desperation makes them
wait, starving, for us
to see through their silence,
to move through this marsh
of our own damned indifference.

James Carroll

LOVE'S POWERS

Deep within us is love—the throbbing life of
the ages;

Love that is of the life that sustains all persons
and wells up within us to flow out into the
common life.

    If two people were to discover together
    this love, the expressiveness of eternity
    would be within each fleeting moment.

If they were to keep discovering that love is
openness toward persons—the doors to and
from the lives of other persons are not locked
. . . the joy, the tragedy, the meaning that
others have fashioned out of their experiences,
all these are welcomed—

    They would be always growing.

    Would words and conversation and acts
    of communion have fresh significance
    —always? Would these two have a
    strange power to bring the distant near,
    and make of the stranger a friend?

And if, in a living way, they now discover that

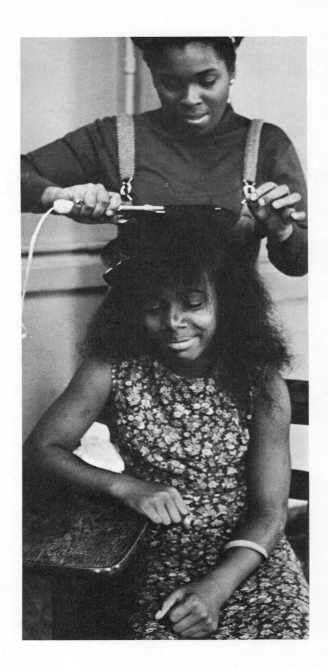

love is creativeness of persons; that is, that love
is participation in the work of a person—creating God,

> Would their lives then acquire a destiny
> and a meaning that is not limited to
> their own threescore years and ten?

If they discover together that love is forgiveness; that evil and sorrow and frustration are
ever battling the sons of men, are never wholly
conquered, but can only be transmuted by a
persistent love that draws us back into fellowship and trust,

> A graciousness, kin to the divine, would
> make their lives a benediction to each
> other and to those about them.

And if, finally, they were to discover that love
is suffering for persons,

> Would they come to have a new ap-
> preciation of Jesus, who died for all men?
> And would the inexhaustible riches of
> Christian love be more desired by them
> than much fine gold?

Ross Snyder

GROWTH IN YOU, O LORD

It was a joy to me, O God, in the midst of the
struggle, to feel that in developing myself
I was increasing the hold that You have upon me;
it was a joy to me, too, under the inward pressure
of life or amid the favourable play of events
to abandon myself to Your Providence. Now that I
have found the joy of utilizing all forms of
growth to make You, or to let You, grow
in me, grant that I may willingly consent to this
last phase of communion in the course of which
I shall possess You by diminishing in You.

After having perceived You as: He who is
'a greater myself,' grant, when my hour comes,
that I may recognise You under the species
of such alien or hostile force that seems bent
upon destroying or supplanting me. When the
signs of age begin to mark my body (and still more
when they touch my mind); when the ill that
is to diminish me or carry me off strikes from
without or is born within me; when the painful moment comes in which I suddenly awaken
to the fact that I am ill or growing old;
and above all at that last moment when I feel
I am losing hold of myself and am absolutely
passive within the hands of the great unknown
forces that have formed me; in all those dark
moments, O God, grant that I may understand
that it is You (provided only my faith is strong
enough) who are painfully parting the fibres of
my being in order to penetrate to the very marrow
of my substance and bear me away within
Yourself.

The more deeply and incurably the evil
is encrusted in my flesh, the more it will be
You that I am harbouring—You as a loving,
active principle of purification and detachment.
The more the future opens before me like some
dizzy abyss or dark tunnel, the more confident
I may be—if I venture forward on the strength

70

of Your word—of losing myself and surrendering myself in You, of being assimilated by Your body, Jesus.

You are the irresistible and vivifying force, O Lord, and because Yours is the energy, because, of the two of us, You are infinitely the stronger, it is on You that falls the part of consuming me in the union that should weld us together. Vouchsafe, therefore, something more precious than the grace for which all the faithful pray. It is not enough that I should die while communicating. Teach me to communicate while dying.

Teilhard de Chardin

My response is painfully clear—it actually hurts to think of what You ask. You say, "Love Me, and I am all mankind." Take the hungry—if I am doing nothing for all the hungry in the world, I am leaving You hungry. And if I leave You hungry, do I love You?

JOY

You can have all sorts of things without love, but you can't have joy.

Sebastian O. Moore

Yes, teach me to respond to Your love. To become more and more aware of Your great love for me, and to become more and more aware of the great possibility of my loving others as You love me.

There is a lack of joy in my life, an unrest, a feeling of incompleteness—is this a sign of my lack of love?

LET US GIVE THANKS

We thank you,
Lord God almighty,
for you are a God of men,
for you are not ashamed
to be called our God,
for you know us all by name
for you hold the world in your hands.
And that is why you have created us
and for this purpose called us into life
that we should be all made one with you
to be your people here on earth.
Blessed are you,
creator of all that is,
blessed are you
for giving us a place of freedom and of life,
blessed are you
for the light of our eyes
and for the air we breathe.

We thank you for the whole of creation,
for all the works of your hands,
for all that you have done among us
through Jesus Christ, our Lord.
Therefore, together with all the living
and all who have gone before us in faith,
we praise your name,
O Lord our God,
bowing before you
adoring you, saying:

   Holy, holy, holy
   Lord of all powers.
   Heaven and earth
   are full of your glory.
   Come and deliver us,
   Lord most high.
   Blessed is he who comes
   in the name of the Lord.
   Come and deliver us,
   Lord most high.

We thank you, holy father,
Lord our God,
for the sake of Jesus Christ,
your beloved son,
whom you called and sent
to serve us and give us light,
to bring your kingdom
to the poor,
to bring redemption
to all captive people
and to be for ever
and for all mankind
the likeness and the form
of your constant love and goodness.
We thank you
for this unforgettable man
who has fulfilled everything
that is human—

our life and death.
We thank you
because he gave himself,
heart and soul, to this world.
For, on the night that he was delivered up,
he took bread into his hands
and raising his eyes to you,
God, his almighty father,
he gave thanks
and broke the bread
and gave it to his friends
with the words:
take and eat,
this is my body for you.
Do this in memory of me.

He also took the chalice
and, giving thanks to you, said:
this chalice is the new covenant in my blood
shed for you and for all mankind
so that sins may be forgiven.
Every time you drink this chalice,
you will do it in memory of me.

So whenever we eat of this bread
and drink from this chalice,
we proclaim the death of the Lord
until he comes.

Therefore, Lord our God,
we present this sign of our faith
and therefore we call to mind
the suffering and death of your son,
his resurrection from the dead,
his entry into your glory,
recalling that he
who is exalted at your right hand
will intercede for us
and that he will come
to do justice to the living and the dead
on the day that you have appointed.

We beseech you
send over us your Holy Spirit
and give a new face
to this earth that is dear to us.
May there be peace
wherever people live,
the peace that we cannot make ourselves
and that is more powerful than all violence,
your peace like a bond,
a new covenant between all men,
the power of Jesus Christ
here among us.

Then your name will be made holy,
Lord our God,
through him and with him and in him
everywhere on earth
and in this fellowship of the Holy Spirit
this hour and every day
world without end.
Amen.

Huub Oosterhuis

*Let us give thanks for this vision of the world and
man in the world with Christ. We can see a new
world-face: peace and love for the poor, the captive,
and all humans. This is the challenge of each Mass:
to build up this new world. But would not the
greatness of the vision be an awesome burden if
You did not share with us the power of Christ? If
Christ did not call His workers together at His
table of love?*

WITHIN

The way of quiet and grateful joy may also lead
to our discovery of the love of God dwelling
within us.

Karl Rahner

I should be joyful in gratitude for the chance to
love and further joyful because of the power of
God's love within me.

ST. PAUL—FAITH, HOPE, LOVE

Though I speak with the tongues of angels, the
tongues of one blessed with many talents and
knowledge but have not Christly love and
understanding of those less blessed than I, I am
no better than a sounding brass.

Though I have gifts from God of various kinds and
have understanding of all kinds of problems and
am "up" on everything, but if I have not the love
of Christ in my heart, I am as clashing cymbals . . .

Though I attend through obligation, and do not
eat meat on Friday, and say some prayers in
times of distress but do nothing because of love
of Christ in my heart, it means not a thing.

I may have all the knowledge, may wear myself
out doing many things, but if I give not love and
do not teach others to love by and through love,
it goes for nothing.

Charity is patient with mistakes of others whether
the mistakes be large or small; whether the
people making the mistakes be other teens, parents,
or teachers.

Charity is understanding the problems of other
teens and giving of my time and convenience
to help them with their problems.

Charity is kind to the teen smarter than I; to the
one less talented than I; to the one that trips all
over trying to dance; to the one who makes
remarks about my appearance or the appearance
of others.

Charity feels no envy for the classmate who gets
a special job; who is publicly praised while I sit
in the background; for the ones who get the
cheerleading jobs, the queen of the prom, the
student council, the class president.

Charity is never perverse or proud with a fellow
classmate who is boring or uninteresting; with a
fellow teen who cannot do as much as I; with the
parent who misunderstands; with the teacher
who messes things up.

Charity writes the note of encouragement to the
teen in sorrow; charity smiles across the study
hall; charity greets all with a cheery hello; charity
laughs and smiles at a joke well told.

Charity will not be provoked by inconstancy of
brothers or sisters, mother or father, teacher or
priest; charity does not brood over changes in
class schedules or a date that did not come off
or a dress not pressed just right or a cafeteria
lunch that doesn't look good.

Charity takes no pleasure in speaking of the
scandals among the student body or their families;
but rejoices in their joys—the new boyfriend or
girlfriend, the new classmate, the new hit record,
the increase in allowance, the acceptance in a
college, the scholarship, the high mark in the exam.

Charity sustains unity; charity listens–to the joyful story and the sad story of a fellow teen; charity rejoices in the gratitude of realizing that I am an instrument of Christ.

THERE IS FAITH—in the vision of the unique dignity of the good each person has.
THERE IS HOPE—in that Christ is in each crying out to the Christ in me.
THERE IS LOVE—an encounter with Christ as He passes through me to others; a love that reaches out to embrace the whole world of teens and adults; and even small children.

Anonymous

St. Paul spoke stern words and I see them well applied here. Love is serious, love is hard. It's very easy to talk a good game, even to go through the right motions; but to really love others, to put them absolutely first—that's tough. But this is the vision that Christ holds out to me. Do I believe Him enough to try to love?

LORD, SECURE JUSTICE

O, Lord, why did you make this world so big?
Only giants could live here rightly,
and we are not giants
but only a people of common size.
We are deathly afraid, Lord,
for everywhere there are powers
of oppression and hunger and war;
We are deathly afraid, Lord,
for we are clothed in those powers
ourselves; we are oppressors.
Yet we would be otherwise.
We would have justice for all,
for our own poor and others.
We would have ample food

for everyman and opportunity,
the food of every human spirit.
We know that we must love
each other or die.
Yet we are in business as usual,
pushing our boulders uphill,
pursuing all kinds of small 'g' gods.
We know it, Lord as a people
that we are by indifference, default,
a race of oppressors, slayers perhaps.
We would like to be a flame
of hope, affirmation, justice.
But we too are victims,
we too are oppressed, slayed men.
We are beaten by ourselves and
some nameless thing more and,
as we say, we are not giants.
So everyone suffers, though we, perhaps, less.
We rise for this moment at least
above the obscuring dust and smoke
of our busy-ness to You.
We hand this worry for the
course of our world
over to You, God, our Father,
for you have promised
to secure justice for the oppressed.
You are the only giant, God.
We men of common size
accept responsibility for this
world and all its victims,
but we do so, we will try,
only because we believe your Word
that justice is your Work
and that in your strength,
through our common weakness
we can do better, perhaps best.

James Carroll

TO SEEK A NEWER WORLD

If you fly in a plane over Europe, toward
Africa or Asia, in a few hours you will cross
over oceans and countries that have been a
crucible of human history. In minutes you
will trace the migration of men over thousands of
years; seconds, the briefest glimpse, and you
will pass battlefields on which millions of men
once struggled and died. You will see no national
boundaries, no vast gulfs or high walls dividing
people from people; only nature and the works
of man—homes and factories and farms—everywhere reflecting man's common effort to enrich
his life. Everywhere new technology and communications bring men and nations closer together,
the concerns of one more and more becoming
the concerns of all. And our new closeness is
stripping away the false masks, the illusion of
difference that is at the root of injustice and hate
and war. Only earthbound man still clings to the
dark and poisoning superstition that his world
is bounded by the nearest hill, his universe ended
at river shore, his common humanity enclosed
in the tight circle of those who share his town
and views and the color of his skin.

Each nation has different obstacles and different
goals, shaped by the vagaries of history and
experience. Yet as I talk to young people around
the world I am impressed not by the diversity but
by the closeness of their goals, their desires and
concerns and hope for the future. There is dis-
crimination in New York, apartheid in South
Africa, and serfdom in the mountains of Peru.
People starve in the streets of India; intellectuals
go to jail in Russia; thousands are slaughtered
in Indonesia; wealth is lavished on armaments
everywhere. These are differing evils, but they
are the common works of man. They reflect the
imperfection of human justice, the inadequacy
of human compassion, the defectiveness of our

sensibility toward the sufferings of our fellows; they mark the limit of our ability to use knowledge for the well-being of others. And therefore, they call upon common qualities of conscience and of indignation, a shared determination to wipe away the unnecessary sufferings of our fellow human beings at home and around the world.

Our answer is the world's hope; it is to rely on youth—not a time of life but a state of mind, a temper of the will, a quality of the imagination, a predominance of courage over timidity, of the appetite for adventure over the love of ease. The cruelties and obstacles of this swiftly changing planet will not yield to obsolete dogmas and outworn slogans. It cannot be moved by those who cling to a present that is already dying, who prefer the illusion of security to the excitement and danger that come with even the most peaceful progress. It is a revolutionary world we live in; and this generation, at home and around the world, has had thrust upon it a greater burden of responsibility than any generation that has ever lived.

"There is," said an Italian philosopher, "nothing more difficult to take in hand, more perilous to conduct, or more uncertain in its success than to take the lead in the introduction of a new order of things." Yet this is the measure of the task of this generation, and the road is strewn with many dangers.

First is the danger of futility, the belief that there is nothing one man or one woman can do against the enormous array of the world's ills— against misery and ignorance, injustice and violence. Yet many of the world's great movements, of thought and action, have flowed from the work of a single man. A young monk began the Protestant Reformation, a young general extended an empire from Macedonia to the borders of the earth, and a young woman reclaimed the territory of France. It was a young Italian explorer who discovered the New World, and the thirty-two-year-old Thomas Jefferson who proclaimed that all men are created equal. "Give me a place to stand," said Archimedes, "and I will move the world."

These men moved the world, and so can we all. Few will have the greatness to bend history itself, but each of us can work to change a small portion of events, and in the total of all those acts will be written the history of this generation. Thousands of Peace Corps volunteers are making a difference in isolated villages and city slums in dozens of countries. Thousands of unknown men and women in Europe resisted the occupation of the Nazis and many died, but all added to the ultimate strength and freedom of their countries. It is from numberless diverse acts of courage and belief that human history is shaped. Each time a man stands up for an ideal, or acts to improve the lot of others, or strikes out against injustice, he sends forth a tiny ripple of hope, and crossing each other from a million different centers of energy and daring, those ripples build a current that can sweep down the mightiest walls of oppression and resistance.

"If Athens shall appear great to you," said Pericles, "consider then that her glories were purchased by valiant men, and by men who learned their duty." That is the source of all greatness in all societies, and it is the key to progress in our time.

The second danger is that of expediency, of those who say that hopes and beliefs must bend before immediate necessities. Of course, if we would act effectively we must deal with the world as it is. We must get things done. But if there was one thing President Kennedy stood for that touched the most profound feelings of people across the world, it was the belief that idealism, high aspirations, and deep convictions are not incompatible with the most practical and efficient of programs—that there is no basic inconsistency between ideals and realistic possibilities, no separation between the deepest desires of heart and mind and the rational application of human effort to human problems. It is not realistic or hardheaded to solve problems and take action unguided by ultimate moral aims and values. It is thoughtless folly. For it ignores the realities of human faith and passion and belief, forces ultimately more powerful than all the calculations of economists or generals. Of course, to adhere to standards, to idealism, to vision in the face of immediate dangers, takes great courage and self-confidence. But we also know that only those who dare to fail greatly can ever achieve greatly.

It is this new idealism that is also, I believe, the common heritage of a generation that has learned that while efficiency can lead to the camps of Auschwitz or the streets of Budapest, only the ideals of humanity and love can climb the hill to the Acropolis.

A third danger is timidity. Few men are willing to brave the disapproval of their fellows, the censure of their colleagues, the wrath of their society. Moral courage is a rarer commodity than bravery in battle or great intelligence. Yet it is the one essential, vital quality for those who seek to change a world that yields most painfully to change. Aristotle tells us that "at the Olympic games it is not the finest and the strongest men who are crowned, but they who enter the lists. . . . So too in the life of the honorable and the good it is they who act rightly who win the prize." I believe that in this generation those with the courage to enter the moral conflict will find themselves with companions in every corner of the world.

For the fortunate among us, the fourth danger is comfort, the temptation to follow the easy and familiar paths of personal ambition and financial success so grandly spread before those who enjoy the privilege of education. But that is not the road history has marked out for us. There is a Chinese curse that says, "May he live in interesting times." Like it or not, we live in interesting times. They are times of danger and uncertainty, but they are also more open to the creative energy of men than any other time in history. And all of us will ultimately be judged, and as the years pass we will surely judge ourselves, on the effort we have contributed to building a new world society and the extent to which our ideals and goals have shaped that effort.

Our future may lie beyond our vision, but it is not completely beyond our control. It is the shaping impulse of America that neither fate nor nature nor the irresistible tides of history, but the work of our own hands, matched to reason and principle, that will determine destiny. There is pride in that, even arrogance, but there is also experience and truth. In any event, it is the only way we can live.

Robert F. Kennedy

Where do I fit in, Lord? Where do You come in? Do You? Can I move the world? Even You seem to fail in that! And it's difficult, it is very difficult to travel the road of the idealist. Maybe to begin is to move! Help me to begin, Lord.

THIS IS MY BODY

In early apostolic times the Eucharist was received at the agape, the community love feast. But these dinners at Corinth were marred by factions, with divisions developing between one group and another, between rich and poor, between the well fed and the hungry. It seems that they—like ourselves—realized only imperfectly the nature of the sacrament that Christ founded at the Last Supper. If we are to think less of the accidentals that separate us, we will have to concentrate in prayer on the great mystery of our supernatural unity—with the body and blood of the Lord making us one with him and one with one another.

1 Cor.
Lord, I confess in sorrow and shame
11:18 that often **when we assemble as a church, there are divisions among us . . .**
20 So that **when we meet together, it is not really your supper that we eat**
for we do not have enough love in our hearts.

23 The account that Paul **received from you, Lord, which he also delivered to us, is that on the night you were betrayed you took bread**
24 **and when you had given thanks, you broke it, and said:**
"This is my body
which is for you.
Do this in remembrance of me."
25 **In the same way also the cup, after supper, saying:**
"This cup is the new covenant in my blood.
Do this, as often as you drink it, in remembrance of me."
26 **For as often as we eat this bread and drink the cup,**
we proclaim your death, O Lord, until you come.
27 **Whoever, therefore, eats the bread or drinks your cup in an unworthy manner will be guilty of profaning your body and blood.**
28 Help me, then, **to examine myself, and so eat of the bread and drink of the cup,** that I may be made worthy to become one with you and one with my neighbor.

Paul Hilsdale

THE GOSPELS

To read the Gospels with faith is to believe . . . everything in them is actually happening now . . . a book of discovery.

Louis Evely

Even at the banquet of the Lord our weakness is evident. Are we better than these early Christians? Do we even see the factions that are among us and that divide us from one another and from all our neighbors and God? Help me to examine myself and act upon what I see.

URGENT CONCERN

If you strip the Christian message, in terms of practical application, to its core, it can sound pretty obvious: that it is necessary to spend ourselves in the service of others, that this is the only way to happiness, the only way to salvation. This, as someone I was speaking to the other day said, sounds common sense.

But although it is common sense, and this is what Christian morality is about, we must do far more than assent to this proposition. It's not merely a question of saying "Oh yes, I see this and I'm going to apply it in my own life as well as I can." Something much more is needed: there has to be a concern in the very deepest sense—a concern which disturbs us, urges us to do something. We need to see with clarity the terrifying predicament of man in his present situation: the lack of concern for others; the lack of love, and so the lack of peace; the enormous danger that hangs over our heads. And when we do see this, we are bound to feel a terrible sense of urgency, because not enough people see it for the community to which we belong to be transformed in the only way that can save it. Perhaps if we saw with sufficient clarity, we should find ourselves too weak to bear the vision. Yet a degree of this insight into the failure of our generation is essential if we are even to begin to have a specifically Christian outlook on life. Such was the insight of the prophets of the Old Testament; it caused them to say things which risked their lives; it was the insight of the apostles, of St. Paul, and above all, of course, of Christ himself.

And surely this is the meaning of the cross: that once we have seen, we feel an enormous responsibility for the generation to which we belong—a responsibility that compels us to go on, in the face of any opposition.

Sebastian Moore

WHY?

Why is it that so many minds see nothing but the stumbling blocks and wait until they are removed before they look at the reasons?

Teilhard De Chardin

Concern . . . urgency . . . do these words describe my Christianity? But for the Christian this is what life is. St. Paul . . . the prophets . . . can I just begin to desire to be like them? Please, God, disturb me!

Is it because we realize down deep the degree and distance of our call? Does the power and purpose of love paralyze us?

WHAT MAKES YOU HAPPY?

**"How happy are the poor in spirit;
theirs is the kingdom of heaven.
Happy the gentle:
they shall have the earth for their heritage.
Happy those who mourn:
they shall be comforted.
Happy those who hunger and thirst for what
    is right:
they shall be satisfied.
Happy the merciful:
they shall have mercy shown them.
Happy the pure in heart:
they shall see God.
Happy the peacemakers:
they shall be called sons of God.
Happy those who are persecuted in the cause
    of right:
theirs is the kingdom of heaven.**

**"Happy are you when people abuse you and
persecute you and speak all kinds of calumny
against you on my account. Rejoice and be
glad, for your reward will be great in heaven; this
is how they persecuted the prophets before you."**

Gospel of Matthew

*But am I ready for this? Persecution and abuse—
or comfort and affluence? What do I really want?
When I see what love really is, can I honestly ask
God to help me to love?*

THOUGH I AM NEIGHBOR

Though I am neighbor,
And they across the way,
A stone's throw perhaps,
I have never met them that I know,
Nor seen them,
Nor hailed them on the walk.
And often under stars
I pause nostalgic and bewildered
To contemplate lanterned dwellings,
Squared and massive somber,
Tree-fringed in the night,
Looming dark-red orange on deep blue haze
In secretive brick.
Such intricate lanterns,
Fading rectangular from blind to blind,
Reticent.
And I am sad to see the image of my life,
Spent among strangers, my own,
Living it out together,
A stone's throw,
And not to have known.

Alfeo Marze

To discover . . . a new language of God.

Dietrich Bonhoeffer

*How many people do we live with that are
strangers to us? Foreigners . . . black men . . . men
of other religions . . . even friends and family—
how many strangers, estranged by lack of love?*

Discovery

. . . and a new way of acting?

ALL YOU NEED IS LOVE

**People capable of love, under the present system,
are necessarily the exceptions; love is by necessity
a marginal phenomenon in present-day western
society . . . because the spirit of a production-
centered, commodity-greedy society is such that
only the non-conformist can defend himself
successfully against it. Important and radical
changes in our social structure are necessary, if
love is to become a social and not a highly
individualistic, marginal phenomenon.**

Erich Fromm

YOU

**To discover . . . through the loving word of another
. . . his own uniqueness . . . destiny . . . freedom.**

Gabriel Moran

*Am I big enough to want to work for this change?
I could so easily find a comfortable niche in this
social structure. My parents and friends even
expect it perhaps. Can I love them enough to
bring the challenge of this change to their attention
I wonder if I really want to do more than talk
about it, sound impressed by it all, and go on as
before. . . .*

*And to realize that changing social structures are at
root not social technology but that it is I working
for you and You—each unique, each wonderful,
each worth the effort.*

DEATH AND RESURRECTION

With Christ I hang upon the cross, and yet I am alive; or rather, not I; it is Christ that lives in me (Gal. 2: 20). You, by baptism, have been united with his burial, united, too, with his resurrection, through your faith in that exercise of power by which God raised him from the dead (Col. 2:12). How rich God is in mercy, with what an excess of love he loved us! Our sins had made dead men of us, and he, in giving life to Christ, gave life to us too; it is his grace that has saved you; raised us up too, enthroned us too above the heavens, in Christ Jesus (Eph. 2: 4-6).

Risen, then, with Christ, you must lift your thoughts above, where Christ now sits at the right hand of God (Col. 3: 1). We are to share his life, because we have shared his death; if we endure, we shall reign with him (2 Tim. 2: 11-12).

COSMIC DEITY

To discover Christ . . . no longer an object of religion but . . . the Lord of the World.

Dietrich Bonhoeffer

To follow the way of love in the Spirit that we have seen and prayed over seems to be enough to kill us—You ask that much. But Christ has shown the way, that this death is truly life. My weakness must die in the works of love that the strength of Christ can live in me.

I think I begin to see and to want to. And with You, are not all things possible?

PEACE

In every prayer for peace there is a touch of
    blasphemy.
It is as though war were inevitable and only God
    could extricate us.

But we are the warriors, the makers and wagers
    of destruction.
(Not God. Not even "they.")
Perhaps our prayers for peace should be for
    forgiveness.
And perhaps they should be said first to
    our brothers.

For "if you are bringing your offering to the altar
    and there remember that your brother has
    something against you, leave your offering
    there before the altar, go and be reconciled
    with your brother first . . ." (Mt. 5:23).

"Brother, forgive us."
"Brother, help us to understand."
And when to the Lord:
A prayer for courage. Help in living with the truth.
We are brothers who seek to destroy.
But brothers.
Peace is a truth lived.
A prayer for peace is an outstretched hand.
Unarmed.

The Christ you have to deal with is not a weak
person outside you, but a tremendous power
inside you.

2 Corinthians 13.3

PEACE

Where has the peace gone to, Lord?
Where has it gone?
Is it gone forever, Lord?
Did it ever come?
People dying, Lord.
O Lord, they're dying.
The bombs falling, the children crying . . .
    they can't find their mother and their father's
    dead.
Dead, Lord–plowed down.
Down into the ground and his children are
    crying. Crying peace.
Let there be peace!
Let the children sing peace, Lord.
Let the people sing peace, Lord.
Let the soldiers sing peace, Lord.
We're ready for dying, Lord, if there's no other way.
But, Lord, I wouldn't kill a man in a war.
I'd just die believing, Lord—and struggling
    and loving.
Die with my children and my woman, Lord;
    that's how I'd die.
But I fear dying like that, Lord,
    because people would say it didn't make sense.
No sense, they would say, Lord.
They'd say I was no man, dying like that with
    my children and my woman, Lord.
That's what they would say.

Would you know, Lord?
I know you would know. Peace!
Amen.

Robert Castle

*We've heard much about "just wars" and how
every man would have been willing to fight and
kill against a Hitler. But when it is all over and
after many centuries of war, one has to ask: Is war
worth the effort? What does killing accomplish?*

CHRISTIAN INVOLVEMENT

Man was put on this earth as scripture tells us not
to leave things the way they were—God created
Adam and he put him in the garden to take
care of it—man is supposed to transform his
world so that it bears a mark of his own intelligence
and his own art and his own concern, because
only if that is there can there be a Christian
dimension to all this. If the world is going to be
Christianized it automatically means to be
humanized.

Bernard Cooke

*If we do not have peace, if we are not at peace,
is it because we have failed to transform our world,
because we have not put our human mark on the
world of our times? This is the service You ask of
us as Christians.*

YOUR PEACE

**+Grant us, O Lord,
a sign of life,
show us, O God,
how much we mean to you.
Come into our world
with your word of creation.
Make us fit to receive you
and grant us your peace.**

Huub Oosterhuis

*Let me never forget that although this work is
mine, it cannot be done without You or unless it
is according to Your creative Word.*

OFFER YOUR GIFT

**It is necessary . . . to take power away from the
privileged minority and give it to the poor majority.
This, if it is done quickly, is the heart of a
revolution. The revolution can be peaceful if the
minority does not resist with violence. The
revolution is, therefore, the way to get a government which will feed the hungry, clothe the naked,
teach the ignorant, comply with the works of
charity, and make possible a true love for our
neighbors. This is why the revolution is not
only permitted but is obligatory for all Christians
who see in it the most effective way of making
possible a greater** love for all men. **It is true that
"there is no authority except that which comes
from God" (St. Paul, Romans, XIII, 1). But
St. Thomas says that, in the practical order,
authority is given by the people.**

When there is an authority which is against the people, that authority is not legitimate and it is called a tyranny. As Christians we can and must fight against tyranny. Our present government is tyrannical because it is supported by only 20 percent of the electorate, and because decisions are made by the privileged minority.

The temporal defects of the Church must not scandalize us. The Church is human. What is important is to believe that it is also divine, and that if as Christians we comply with our obligation to love our neighbor by so doing we are reinforcing the Church.

I have put aside the privileges and duties of the clergy, but I have not stopped being a priest. I think I have given myself to the revolution out of love for my neighbor. I have stopped offering Mass to live out the love for my neighbor in the temporal, economic, and social orders. When my neighbor no longer has anything against me, and when the revolution has been completed, then I will offer Mass again, if God so wills it. I believe that in this way I am following Christ's injunction. "If you bring your offering to the altar and there remember that your brother has something against you, leave your offering on the altar and go and be reconciled first with your brother, and then return and offer your gift" (St. Matthew, V, 23-24).

After the revolution we Christians will have the peace of mind which will come from knowing that we established a system which is grounded in the love of neighbor.

The struggle will be long. Let us begin today. . . .

Camilo Torres

Is not Camilio Torres' country much like ours? We too have a "revolution" to perform, that of bringing American society to a social order dominated by concern for neighbor above all else. Will there be any peace for us that is not a product of this struggle?

JUSTICE

Peace will not come out of a clash of arms, but out of justice lived and done by unarmed nations in the face of odds.

Gandhi

Again the words of a great man bring us up short. Does self-defense mean as much as other-justice?

4TH OF JULY ORATION

For the present it is enough to affirm the equal manhood of the Negro race. Is it not astonishing that, while we are plowing, planting, and reaping, using all kinds of mechanical tools, erecting houses, constructing bridges, building ships, working in metals of brass, iron, copper, silver and gold; that while we are reading, writing, and cyphering, acting as clerks, merchants and secretaries, having among us lawyers, doctors, ministers, poets, authors, editors, orators, and teachers; that while we are engaged in all the enterprises common to other men—digging gold in California, capturing the whale in the Pacific, feeding sheep and cattle on the hillside, living, moving, acting, thinking, planning, living in families as husbands, wives, and children, and above all, confessing and worshipping the Christian God, and looking hopefully for life and immortality beyond the grave—we are called upon to prove that we are men?

Frederick Douglass 1852

The sin-seeds of the violence that disturb our peace today have been sown long ago. Can we expect anything but a bitter harvest? In the face of such a stubborn growth can we work to remove it halfheartedly?

JUNGLE GAMES

The children laughed
their village games
within flowers until
silver birds flicked

fire and dropped
scorching jelly.

Children, children,
forgive them their flames.
They know not the hurt
they do with their games.

Robert Haiduke

This is the face of war—what make-up will we need to make it a face of peace?

UNTO DEATH

In the year 6 B.C., a man was born who was more than a man. His human nature was sustained in existence and made to be a person by the indwelling personality of the Eternal Word of God. In all right and justice, human nature raised to this undreamed-of excellence should have been shot through with glory, honor, and immortality. But for our sake Christ preferred to be without these divine prerogatives for a time, choosing instead to live for thirty-three long years a life of service and obscurity. It was by veiling his divine glory that he unveiled ("revealed") for all time the consuming nature of divine love. Still, the glory could not remain covered. His mission on earth accomplished, he received from his heavenly Father the Name, that is the visible authority and excellence, of the divinity.

Phil.

2:2 May we learn to **be of the same mind,**
having the same love,

3 Teach us to **do nothing from selfishness**
or conceit;
but in humility
to count others better than ourselves.

4 **Let each of us**
look not only to our own interests,
but also to the interests of others.

In other words, Lord, give us your mind.

6 For you, **though you were in the form of God,**
did not count equality with God
a thing to be grasped;

7 **but you emptied yourself,**
taking the form of a servant,
being born in the likeness of men.

8 **And being found in human form**
you humbled yourself
and became obedient unto death
even death on a cross.

9 **That is why your Father has highly exalted**
you
and bestowed on you the name
which is above every name.
And that is why in your presence

10 **every knee should bow,**
in heaven and on earth and under the earth,

11 **and every tongue should confess**
that you, Jesus Christ, are Lord,
to the glory of your Father in heaven.

Paul Hilsdale

*How could there be war if we all looked to one
another's interests? You allowed Your Son to walk
among us just to look to our interests and help us.
Who is Christ but the man who came to help? Who
is a Christian . . .?*

WHAT WAS HIROSHIMA LIKE, JESUS, WHEN THE BOMB FELL?

What went through the minds of mothers,
what happened to the lives of children,
what stabbed at the hearts of men when they
were caught up in a sea of flames?

What was Auschwitz like, Jesus, when the
crematoriums belched the stinking smoke from the
burned bodies of people? When families were
separated, the weak perished, the strong faced
inhuman tortures of the spirit and the body. What
was the concentration camp like, Jesus?

Tell us, Lord, that we, the living, are
capable of the same cruelty, the same horror,
if we turn our back on you, our brother, and
our other brothers. Save us from ourselves;
spare us the evils of our hearts' good intentions,
unbridled and mad. Turn us from our perversions
of love, especially when these are perpetrated
in your name. Speak to us about war, and about
peace, and about the possibilities for both
in our very human hearts.

Malcolm Boyd

*Help me to remove my American blinders. The
Germans were butchers, the Japanese cruel, but
not us. . . . Hiroshima . . . Nagasaki . . . Hamburg
. . . Dresden . . . first use of atom bomb . . . fire
bombing . . . When will we ever learn?*

THE SPIRIT

A decisive hour will sound for mankind, when
the spirit of discovery absorbs . . . the spirit of war.

Teilhard De Chardin

Will that be in our lifetime? Why shouldn't it be?

DEATH IS A BUTTON

Death is the result of all this button-pushing, but
it's down there at the other end—mere dots on
a map. But these pilots have no contact with
the blood or the dust; they don't hear one
groan, one call for help. They have no contact with
the corpses of men, women and children blown
apart or burned to a cinder down below. That is,
unless anti-aircraft turns them into corpses like
the other corpses. But that's a hazard of their
profession which they accept along with the pay,
as in any other profession.

If these pilots make it through their mission
safely, they return to the base to eat, drink,
relax, and perhaps go to church on Sunday to hear
a sermon on the text: "Blessed are the meek.
Blessed are the compassionate. Blessed are the
peaceful."

The truth, of course, is that these pilots are
just average people—like the large majority of
people on this earth. No better, no worse.
The profession of a military pilot is just a job,
another "honest" way of making a living.

Motive

And for us death is a newspaper story or a T.V. report. Oh, yes, the blood looks bad on our color set, but no worse than Bullitt or many a movie we have seen. Many die every night on show after show—maybe the Vietnam news is just Southeast Asian Bonanza?

LITANY OF THE DESOLATE NATION

Leader: **Our nation is moving toward two societies, one black, one white—separate and unequal.**

People: **"If a house is divided against itself, that house will not be able to stand."**

Leader: **Our present system of public welfare is designed to save money instead of people, and tragically ends up doing neither.**

People: **"There will be no poor among you if only you will obey the voice of the Lord your God and do his commandments."**

Leader: **During the first quarter of the twentieth century, the federal government enacted no new legislation to ensure equal rights . . . and despite flagrant violations made little attempt to enforce existing laws.**

People: **"Its rulers give judgment for a bribe, its priests teach for hire, its prophets divine for money, saying, 'No evil shall come upon us.' "**

Leader: **In three decades federal subsidy has built eight hundred thousand housing units for the disadvantaged; federal mortgage**

guarantees have made possible over
ten million middle and upper income units.

People: "Woe to those who lie upon beds of ivory
and anoint themselves with the finest
oils, but are not grieved over the
ruin of Joseph!"

Leader: The atmosphere of hostility and cynicism
is reinforced by a widespread belief
that there is a double standard of
justice and protection.

People: "The prince and the judge ask for a bribe,
and the great man utters the evil desire of
his soul; thus they weave it together."

Leader: In World War II the Red Cross, with
government approval, in blood banks
for wounded servicemen, separated
Negro and white blood.

People: "God made of one blood every nation of
men to live on all the face of the earth."

Leader: Vietnam diverted the attention of the
country from the issue of equality.

People: "You have shed much blood and have
waged great wars; you shall not build a
house to my name because you have
shed so much blood."

Leader: We have seen in our cities a chain reaction of racial violence: If we are heed-
less, none of us shall escape the conse-
quences.

People: "Because you trusted in your strongholds
and your treasures, you also shall be

taken; the destroyed shall come upon
every city, and no city shall escape."

Leader: Weapons which are designed to destroy,
not to control, have no place in
densely populated communities.

People: "Put your sword back in its place; for all
who take the sword will perish by the
sword."

Leader: Observers report that city fathers seemed
unaware of the seriousness of the tensions.

People: "Lord, when did we see thee hungry-or
thirsty or a stranger or naked or
sick or in prison?"

Leader: The major need is to generate new will—
the will to tax ourselves to the extent
necessary to meet the vital needs
of the nation.

People: "I will buy it for a price; I will not offer to
the Lord that which costs me nothing."

Leader: For every American the situation requires
new attitudes, new understanding,
and, above all, new will.

People: "Repent and turn from all your transgressions, lest iniquity be your ruin. Cast
away all your transgressions which you
have committed, and get yourselves
a new heart and a new spirit! For I have
no pleasure in the death of anyone, says
the Lord: so turn, and live."

National Council of Churches

*Vietnam is not the real problem—it is in our cities,
our universities, our homes, our streets. We must
truly turn from the evil way of selfishness, neglect,
lack of interest, and comfort at all costs. Help us
to live the way of active concern for justice, for
harmony, for understanding, for opportunity. Give
us peace.*

INSTRUMENT
OF THY
PEACE

Lord, make me an instrument of Thy peace. Where
there is hatred, let me sow love; where there
is injury, pardon; where there is doubt, faith;
where there is despair, hope; where there is sadness
joy; where there is darkness, light.

O Divine Master, grant that I may not so much
seek to be consoled, as to console; not so much to
be understood, as to understand; not so much
to be loved, as to love. For it is in giving that we
receive, it is in pardoning that we are pardoned, it
is in dying that we are born again to eternal life.

St. Francis of Assisi

*Can I make this more than a prayer for peace?
Can I make it a promise of work for peace? Can I
make it?*

SEQUEIROS' ECHO OF A SCREAM

A baby sits alone in the war-rubble of a field
Screaming. Behind the baby's head
An exact copy of the same screaming head,
Four times enlarged.

"An agonized protest against wars
That bomb babies and destroy civilizations."
                                    (Sarah Newmeyer)

  "An infant's most despairing cry
  Is not when he feels physical pain
  But when he feels himself abandoned."
                                    (Louis Lavelle)

"Why, the whole world of the knowledge
Of good and evil
Is not worth that child's prayer
To 'dear, kind God'
To protect her."
                                    (Feodor Dostoyevski)

  Jesus Christ, if you had not cried
  "My God, my God,
  Why hast Thou forsaken me?"
  I would be an atheist.

Thomas R. Heath, O.P.

*We rationalize war and tell ourselves that for many
noble reasons we must kill and fight—and still that
baby's head haunts us. What are we to do?*

CONTEMPLATIVE LIFE

The term "contemplative life" is one that is much
mistreated. It is more often used than defined,
and that is why arguments about the respective
merits of "active" and "contemplative" orders
generally end nowhere. . . . I am not talking about
the contemplative orders, but about the
contemplative life. It is a life that can be led and,
in fact, must eventually be led by every good
Christian. It is the life for which we were created,
and which will eventually be our everlasting joy in
heaven. By the grace of Christ we can begin
to lead that life even on earth, and many in fact
do so begin. Some of them are in cloisters,
because the vows and rules of religious orders and
congregations make the necessary work of
preparation easy and, as it were, almost a matter
of course. But many more "contemplatives" are out
in the world. A lot of them may be found
in places like Harlem and wherever people suffer,
and perhaps many of these have never even heard
the word "contemplative." And yet, on the other
hand, not all of those who are in contemplative
orders are contemplatives. Through their own
fault they miss the end of their vocation. . . .

Thomas Merton

*What is a contemplative? Is he not one who ponders
his world, listens for Your voice, and follows what
he hears?*

EMPTY

To a man with an empty stomach, food is God.

Gandhi

To a man with an empty heart, is not loving concern God?

TRANSFIGURATION

May God become God for us once again!
Let's allow Him to be for us what He really is:
        all love and thoughtfulness,
        our vocation and our reward;
let's allow Him at last to show us His true face,
    instead of the dark, joyless mask we've painted
    Him.
      He invites us every day
        to this illuminating discovery,
        this transfiguration.

Louis Evely

You invite us to illuminate this world, to discover its meaning, and transform its absurdity. Will we? Dare we?

BUDDHIST NON-VIOLENCE

"I will protect myself" thus the Foundations of Mindfulness have to be cultivated. "I will protect others" thus the Foundations of Mindfulness have to be cultivated. *By protecting oneself one is protecting others; by protecting others one is protecting oneself.*

    And how does one by protecting oneself protect others? By repeated practice, by meditative culture of mind and by frequent occupation with it.

    And how does one by protecting others protect oneself? By patience, by a non-violent life, by loving-kindness and compassion.

Nayanaponika Thera

Is there any other meaning to self-defense?

NAPALM
(a cinquain poem)

How sad
to think that you
will not sing again your
song of innocence, without fear
of fire.

Robert Haiduke

How sad . . . how real . . . how terrible. . . .

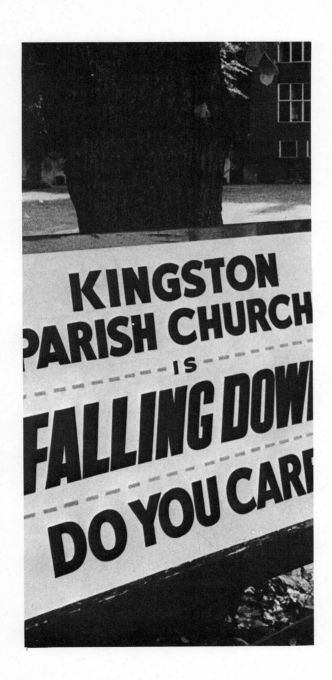

GOD'S PRESENCE

We're glad we can think
You are a father
Maybe like we wish we got.

We are happy
That you will stay around.
Just thinking about that
Makes us feel just great.

Carl Burke

We have a Father—do we have any brothers?

THE SECOND ADAM

Selfishness, sin and suffering
are man's doing, not yours, O God.
Sin came into the world through one man
and death through him,
and so death spread to all men
because all men sinned . . .

Many died through one man's trespass;
But this, I firmly believe, is but a shadow
of the great positive fact that
the grace of one man—you, Lord Jesus Christ—
has abounded for many.
And your free gift
is not like the effect of that one man's sin.
For the judgment following one trespass
brought condemnation,
but the free gift following many trespasses
brings justification.

If, because of one man's trespass,
death reigned through one man,

much more
will those who receive the abundance of grace
and the free gift of righteousness
reign in life
through one man
        who came to redeem us:
        You, my Lord and Savior,
            Jesus Christ.

By one man's disobedience
many were made sinners,
so by one man's obedience
many will be made righteous . . .
Where sin increased,
grace abounded all the more,
so that as sin reigned
and brought death to body and soul,
grace also might reign
through righteousness,
bringing eternal life
through you, Jesus Christ our Lord.

Epistle to the Romans

*But grave though our situation is, though peace
be banished from our midst, still You through
Your Son make our situation possible. You are not
banished from our midst, and if we will, we
can. Send us the help of Your peace, help us
send Your peace to the world.*

REGARD

We must learn to regard people less in the light of what they do or omit to do, and more in the light of what they suffer.

Dietrich Bonhoeffer

And even those who fail to be peace-makers must still be regarded with Christ's love—for there is no other way.

A PRAYER OF DISCIPLESHIP

"Send me."

But where, Lord? To do what?

To bring pardon where there had been injury in a life I casually brush against at my daily work? (But I had thought of mediating a teenage gang war in Chicago!)

To help turn doubt into faith in a person with whom I live intimately in my circle of family or friends? (But I had thought of helping a tired drunk on skid row!)

To bring joy into a life, consumed by sadness, which touches the hem of my life at a drinking fountain? (But I had thought only of a far-off mission land!)

"Send me." Send me next door, into the next room, to speak somehow to a human heart beating alongside mine. Send me to bear a note of dignity into a subhuman, hopeless situation. Send me to show forth joy in a moment and a place where there is otherwise no joy but only the will to die.

Send me to reflect your light in the darkness of futility, mere existence, and the horror of casual human cruelty. But give me your light, too, Lord, in my own darkness and need.

Malcolm Boyd

I think I am ready. It will not be easy—but this is the only way to be that more that freedom and love allow me. Give me Your light but never lighten my burden, for is not my burden my self?

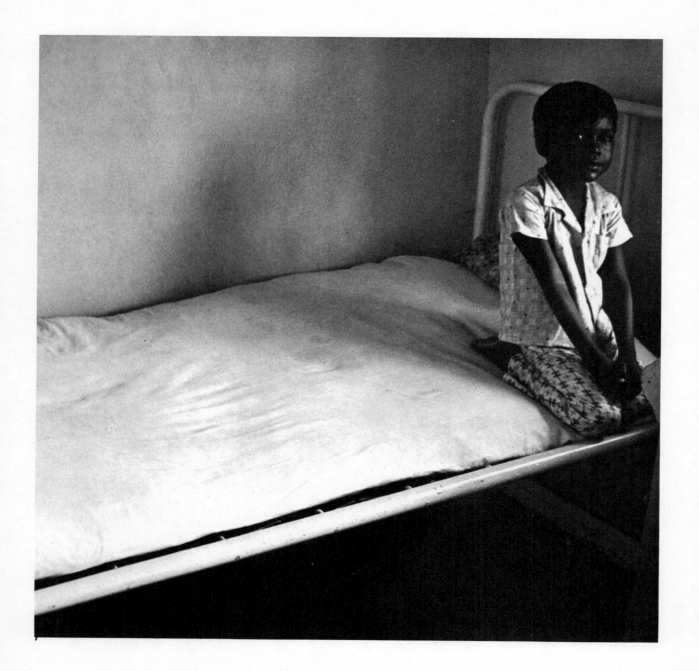

LIFE

Where do I *live?*
A street number is not the answer. Life is not in
  geography.
Where then?
In the unmeasured and undefined?
In a true word, an honest response, in a moment
  without fear?
Maybe the question is wrong?
Maybe it is not "where" but "whether."
Remember the boy, back from the bad trip who
  said: "I was trying to find out if I was alive."
Maybe that's the question.
"Am I?"

The truth is we neither live nor die as self-
contained units. At every moment life links
us to the Lord.

Romans 14: 7-8

A PSALM
FOR THE NEW HUMANITY

*("With the aid of Divine Grace we look forward
to the emergence of men who are truly new
partisans of a new humanity.")*
        —*Pastoral Constitution* Gaudium et Spes

Down the street the sidewalk's glory greets us
with its cracked mother's backs;
The crowd meets feet at corners, talking,
    smoking, walking to school.
        The crowd (not the sidewalks or the corners
        or just the street)
            walk together; only the crowded arms in
            arms or without arms or not in arms
        But some in arms.
The crowd sings (singing full is crowded) love
    is a crowd of two or more
Not three's a crowd; more than that's what's a
    real crowd.
        Catholics, no; whites, no–they're groups,
            not crowds;
        Who's in your crowd? Me? God, it's crowded
            in the city.
Energy crowds atoms and the explosion is
    movement
        Moving through downtown, suburbs,
            history is crowds.
        Christ walked through crowds, is seen
            through crowds
        Twelve or so were in his crowd: internal
            revenue men and mystics;
        Women, too—mothers, real and whore-
            gotten—never out of the crowd, crowded
            out, forgotten.
        But in at His feet at a reserved table, let
            into the in-crowd.
Sunsets reflected on buildings: tens of thousands
    of suns produce a crowd of son suns and
    scream around, thoroughly thoroughfare.

Finest Lord,
    Let us crowd our love
Batter down, weld fast, with fire,
    the fatter than ever feeling of electric
        wires
The flood of your face in our blood.

Fast is quick (L rides are so) fast is sure as; up
    tight; in the go group.
She's fast on the first date if she doesn't wait
    till the third or last.
        She gets there early before the other birds.
        Quick! Sharp! Snap! my stop and off
        (gosh they're fast—never got past the
            second page and we were here).

Time goes fast when we're making love,
        Making it last. It cannot wait. It holds
            us fast together,
        Sealed forever in this moment with the
            quick-lit city of street lights turning
            on at once.
        Children running fast: home   a fast
            make   punch   train   lunch
            twist   one kiss   sky   all fast
        tight for men.

Finest Lord,
    Let us crowd our love
Batter down, weld fast, with fire,
    the fatter than ever feeling of electric
        wires
The flood of your face in our blood.

Glow of the lake like slow dead fire, hanging, and
    then real red in the fog,
        Bright, hot fire of color sneaking through
            higher, higher brother to the shore
Brother elements of earth: heat of sky and soil
    combust and burst into city of men and God;

And riots purified by fire of cars in the park.
Hit by hate
Lit by fear
And burned the Phoenix symbol; left the
     ashes
Destroy and test by fire.
Burning fervor of nuns and others ignite
     the streets;
The crowds held fast by fire;
Hot blaze steel sweats life and breath at
night in the smoked out city of
     lovers and thieves.

Finest Lord,
     Let us crowd our love
Batter down, weld fast, with fire,
     the fatter than ever feeling of electric wires
The flood of your face in our blood.

Welded into crowds by fire are we held fast and
     fast we must be to save the unity so newly
     gotten by a thousand years of Resurrection.
Pushing close, melted into neighborhoods the
     good crowd waits for separation to end,
     Hooked, we hope, on the narcotic dope
          of Christian overbearing Love.
     Bent and shaped, our fate in the moment
          of the fire and the rose.
     The still point of living—the dance and
          dancer—
     Life melded to life nowhere and everywhere
          caught up—
     Once   eternal   met.
Finest Lord,
     Let us crowd our love
Batter down, weld fast, with fire,
     the fatter than ever feeling of electric
          wires
The flood of your face in our blood.

Feeling fat: feeling that spread all out of self.
     Living better electrically
Especially with electricity of simple joy
     to be all over this fat bulged world of
     everybody overweight: expectant,
     pregnant
With offering of solid gold Cadillac, Frank's
     insensitivity and Murphy's fat handshake;
     glad to race in space, to tell
          on the wires of the universe the word
          of themselves and their offspringing
          wells of glory and for the fortieth
          time all from the glorious fat of that
          electric feeling of being big and
          pleasing and all overheated.
     Try it: talking the world out of a diet.

Finest Lord,
     Let us crowd our love
Batter down, weld fast, with fire,
     the fatter than ever feeling of electric wires
The flood of your face in our blood.

The flood chased those who fled him down the
     nights in alleyways and
          Parked cars and cocktail bars and ran
               after them in the days;
     Those who turned away from the water of
          cool, wet glance on their tired throats
          and eyes and limbs:
     Lovely in limbs soaked through by flood
          of being caught in a rain with no coat.
     Rushing in,
          the water seeks in every dry crevice a
               place to seep into, to find
               the face it needs to face with His.
To face the flood needs no little bit of good, red
     blood; but once done
          The brittle bone is faced and wet and gone

110

in lieu of moving and breathing;
The force of that flood pushing in to
    make the bloody beast;
Face divine   kissed   caressed
    laced in its licking tongue.
Hot, wet, fired, fat—bulbous dream of
    faces streamed with tears,
    Watered, it seems, by years of floods and
    faces.
Waves of the white floating Savior's face.
        Baptism (of flood water) in our Blood
        And not in vain our veins are drowned in
            the down poured Christ.

Nancy Gallagher

*The page runs over with the sights and sounds
and smells and symbols of the new humanity. In
this hectic hazardous world we rush forward into
new life and a new community of love. We dream
and hope to body forth Christ as a new wonderful
creature of new life. Can we penetrate our
vision to see the new world of new life breaking
through all around us? Can we see?*

SIN

I have fallen, Lord,
Once more.
I can't go on, I'll never succeed.
I am ashamed, I don't dare look at you.

Lord, I knew you were right near me, bending
     over me, watching;
All I had to do was call.
But temptation blew like a hurricane,
And instead of looking at you I turned my
     head away.
There you stood silent and sorrowful.
There I stood, alone, ashamed, and disgusted.
You loved me and I forgot you.

But you said:
Come son, look up.
Isn't it your pride that is wounded?
If you loved me, you would grieve, but you
     would trust.
Do you think that there is a limit to God's love?
Do you think for a moment that I stopped
     loving you?
But you still rely on yourself, son.
You must rely on me.

Ask my pardon,
And get up quickly.
You see, it's not falling that is the worst,
But staying on the ground.

                                        Amen.

*I do fear to trust You. It is so safe and secure
clinging to the ground and staring in the dirt.
But You hold out a vision and You will not let even
my sin blind me to it.*

BY THEIR VEGETABLES SHALL YOU KNOW THEM

**But really when you think of it,
It's not the stagnant flood of gloom-green
   oh-so-soothing-thick despair
That gets you;**

**It's the good old quite unlovely—and you
   brought it on yourself—
Quick
Daily daytime droplets of hope
   that you—you did!—
Saw (Espied)
And let fall anyhow
To pollute the place you'd been.**

New City

*The moments of true hope come by me day by
day—why do I watch them go by?*

THE MEANING OF RELIGION

**Now that I have turned from the mere outward
"form of religion" to its inner meaning, I find
that it is anything but an opiate of the people.
Religion is not a dreamlike escape from the world;
it is the hard confrontation of created man and
uncreated reality—of darkness and light, of love
and persecution. Fortunately there is a partial road
map to guide my searching steps, the scriptures
which are divinely inspired "for teaching . . . and
for training in righteousness."**

The Meaning of Religion

II Timothy

Lord, I confess that I have been
3:2   **in love with self,
a lover of money,
proud, arrogant, abusive . . . ungrateful . . .**
4   **swollen with conceit,
a lover of pleasure rather than a lover
of God,**
5   **holding the** outward **form of religion
but denying the power of it.**

But now I am trying to lead a better life.
12   And I accept the fact that all **who desire
to live a godly life in you, Christ Jesus,
will be persecuted.**

14   But in spite of this I hope **to continue
in what I have learned
and have firmly believed,
knowing from whom I learned it,**
15   and having **your sacred writings . . .
to instruct me for salvation . . .**
16   **For all scripture
is inspired by you, my God,
and is profitable for teaching,
for reproof, for correction,
and for training in righteousness.**
17   Help me, Lord, to be **a man of God,
complete,
and equipped for every good work.**

Paul Hilsdale

*I have even hidden behind the skirts of religion
rather than face the challenge of the vision You
hold out to me. But Your power pushes me on
to pursue every good work in purchasing a new
humanity. Why do I resist?*

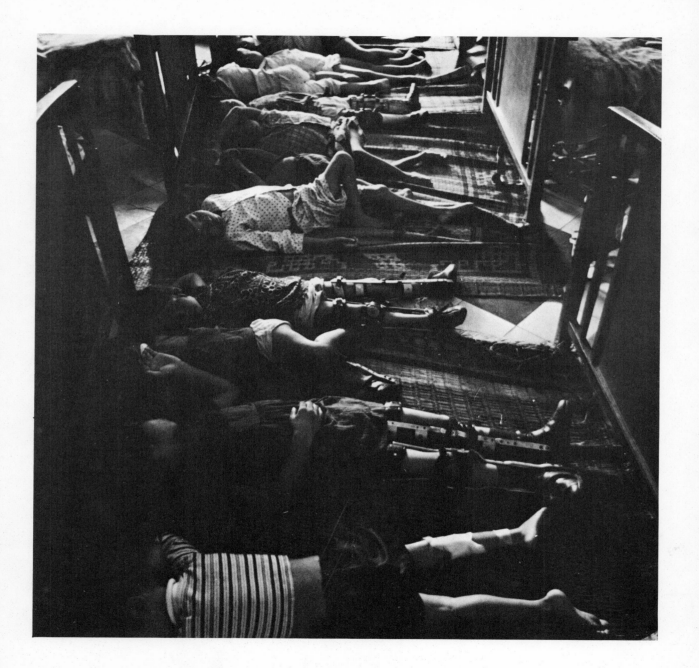

IT'S MORNING, JESUS

It's morning, Jesus it's morning, and
here's that light and sound all
over again.

I've got to move fast . . . get into the bathroom,
wash up, grab a bite to eat, and run some more.

I just don't feel like it, Lord. What I really
want to do is get back into bed, pull up the
covers, and sleep. All I seem to want today is
the big sleep, and here I've got to run all over again.

Where am I running? You know these
things I can't understand. It's not that I need to
have you tell me. What counts most is just that
somebody knows, and it's you. That helps a lot.

So I'll follow along, okay? But lead, Lord.
Now I've got to run. Are you running with me,
Jesus?

Malcolm Boyd

*But I must go on, there is no other way—You will
not allow me to wallow in a comfortable oldness
that stifles the life that is to be.*

CONFESSION OF FAITH

I BELIEVE IN THE LIVING GOD,
FATHER OF JESUS CHRIST OUR LORD,
OUR GOD, OUR ALMIGHTY FATHER.

God who ACTS
        and the fog lifts
or is shattered
        by full-throated
                laughter
Joy growing
through hope's nudging
        rising to crescendo
throughout the world
        HE LIVES!

HE HAS CREATED THE WORLD, ALL
        THINGS
IN HIS ONLY BELOVED SON,
THE IMAGE AND LIKENESS OF HIS GLORY

and flowers
        and rain
                drops
musty smell of hot wetness
and moldy smell of garbage
war
        and tears
and wounded dove
unexpected sun
unwanted cold
        and people
        all people
        God's people
somehow take shape
        kaleidoscope-like
        in His Son

JESUS, LIGHT OF ETERNAL LIGHT,
WORD OF GOD, FAITHFUL, ABIDING,
JESUS CHRIST, OUR GRACE AND OUR
    TRUTH.

Jesus–
    light so intense
      Surfaces peel
      and naked
        reality
      stands bathed
      in His light
Jesus—
    Word straining ever
    to be realized
      to burst out
      SPOKEN
      filling forever
    the hollow silence
      of man

IN ORDER TO SERVE THIS WORLD OF
    OURS,
IN ORDER TO SHARE OUR HUMAN LOT,
HE BECAME FLESH OF OUR HUMAN FLESH.

Oneness in humanity
Tangible evidence of
Divinity's desire to
      BE
    for another

BY THE WILL OF THE HOLY SPIRIT
AND BORN OF THE VIRGIN MARY
HE BECAME MAN, A MAN LIKE US.

. . . a day much like others
    save for the
      breath of the Spirit
      and a virgin's response

The Transcendent is enfleshed
by a woman's
        "yes"

HE WAS BROKEN FOR OUR SINS
AND WAS OBEDIENT UNTO DEATH
AND GAVE HIMSELF UPON THE CROSS.

THEREFORE HE HAS RECEIVED THE NAME
OF THE FIRSTBORN FROM THE DEAD,
THE SON OF GOD AND LORD OF ALL.

Sun
        spread on cross beams
        eclipsed by evil that was
            and will be
        by man's rejection of man
            his indifference
            his pin-head world leaving
                no room for
                    the poor
                    or lonely
                    or useless
A nod to the darkening day
        then light lingers an instant
            and is
                no more

HE WILL COME IN GOD'S OWN TIME
TO DO JUSTICE TO THE LIVING AND THE
        DEAD.
HE IS THE MAN WHOM I SHALL RESEMBLE.

Out of history
        he'll step again
but I in the
            now
            am
        a moon
sharing with its sun
to make the world
        a bit brighter

I BELIEVE IN THE POWER OF THE SPIRIT,
IN THE LOVE OF THE FATHER AND THE
    SON
IN THE COVENANT OF GOD WITH MEN.

Fragmented man beholds
    confusion
    within him and
    without
and cries out
    unknowingly
    yearningly
    for unifying reason
    for a place within the circle
      of Father
        Son
      and Spirit
where the Other
may touch him
    with the integrator–
        Love

IN THE CHURCH, THE BODY OF CHRIST,
CALLED TOGETHER AND SENT FORTH
TO DO THE WORK THAT HE HAS DONE—

TO ENLIGHTEN AND TO SERVE
AND TO BEAR THE SINS OF THE WORLD
AND TO BUILD UP PEACE ON EARTH.

I BELIEVE THAT WE SHALL ARISE
FROM DEATH WITH A NEW, UNDYING
    BODY,
FOR HE IS THE GOD OF THE LIVING.

Reach out! Extend!
    the Spirit urges
and say the Word
        Be
the word

or He remains
     only
a promise.

Now winter's past—
    no shadow remains
       of chilling doubt
        dark isolation
Death's ashes disperse
    with the breath of
      New Life
Spring is eternal
    in Christ-ed man
      AMEN. COME, LORD JESUS, COME.

Sister Athena

*My faith is in the future. Where else could
it be? A new Spring in You who act, in Christ who
speaks, and I your moon who helps. Think of
what my "yes" can do! What could be greater,
what could be more, than saying yes to
Your act and Your Word?*

DISCRIMINATING DISCRIMINATION

How do I know if I am really united with Christ?
How can I measure my love of God? My
Christian neighbor is more Christ than colored,
more Christ than Semite, more Christ than poor.
Do I love my Lord, therefore, when I meet him in
the streets? That is the question; that is the test.

GAL.
3:26 **In you, O Christ,**
we are all sons of the Father
through faith.
27 **For as many of us**
as were baptized into you
have put on your person **O Christ.**

28 **There is neither Jew nor Greek,**
neither white nor colored,
neither slave nor free,
neither rich nor poor,
there is neither male nor female;
for we are all one in you, Lord.
20 **And if we are yours,**
then we are . . . heirs according to promise.
And we look forward to the day of eternity
when we will be with you, and with all
who have been given to share in your life.

Paul Hilsdale

The future we work for is secure because the future
is Christ in whom we all have life and promise.
Can I spare any effort? Dare I use any measure?

GLORIA IN EXCELSIS

Glory to God in heaven,
and peace to his people on earth.

Lord God, heavenly King,
almighty God and Father,
we worship you, we give you thanks,
we praise you for your glory.

Lord Jesus Christ, only Son of the Father,

Lord God, Lamb of God,
you take away the sin of the world:
have mercy on us.

You are seated at the right hand of the Father:
receive our prayer.

For you alone are the Holy One,
you alone are the Lord,
you alone are the Most High,
Jesus Christ,
with the Holy Spirit,
in the glory of God the Father. Amen.

Offically Proposed
Ecumenical Version

Amen. So may it be. So will *it be!*

AMERICAN SUMMER

Re-creation always meant baseball,
Gross National Pastime
Where power and speed are responsible
For Victory: but I could never hit
The ball hard enough, the bat
Was always flying from my hands.
When and if I did connect,
I rarely made it to the base in time.

Geof Hewitt

*But this is a new game in which Christ is
responsible for the Victory. Is there any room for
fear of failure?*

LET'S BE HONEST

—And that is by and large the way people tend
to think of religion as an aspect of life, as something
which they ought to have—you know—to be a
well-rounded person you ought to get an
education, you ought to have some hobbies, you
should have some friends and you should have
a religion.

Let us be honest with ourselves: many of us
have such an attitude, even though there was not
the slightest trace of such a thing in Christ. He
accepted identification with sinners and with
publicans and, if these people came and were open
and accepted him, he never rejected them. And
he did the same with his Apostles. The Apostles
are an interesting group to study. There was
Matthew, a publican, who probably was a fairly
shrewd operator, because he had to live off
the taxes he collected, and did. He was getting
along well enough for prominent people not to
mind being seen with this publican. When he
gave a party, at any rate, to announce his retirement
from the ranks of the publicans to become a
disciple of Christ, apparently some very prominent
people showed up. Then there was someone like
Simon—not the Simon who became Peter, but the
other one who was called a zealot, which means
that he belonged to the extreme right-wing
movement in those days. You had the sons of
Zebedee, John and James, both of them hot-headed
as could be; when things did not go right they
expected the heavens to rain fire and brimstone on
those who rejected them. And of course, there was
Peter himself, a unique figure if any of the
Apostles were.

*Such a comfortable, choked Christianity will never
do. It's not the full and vibrant Christianity
that led such a rich variety of people to Christ and
to His life. Is my Christianity an aspect of a
crowded life or is it life itself?*

TOO MUCH MONEY

Tell them too much money has killed men
And left them dead years before burial

Carl Sandburg

*How many things try to choke the life that is
Christ. Why do I prefer money and things to
Christ and life?*

CREATIVITY

His encounter with his surroundings is meant to be
a creative process in which both they and he
are fulfilled. This means that the world of man
is essentially open to change. It is there to be
transformed, not merely endured. Like the artist
struggling with a stubborn medium, whose
possibilities he can only gradually realize and
never exhaust, man is called continually to grapple
with the world around him with a view to its
endless enhancement.

Robert O. Johann

This is life! The struggle to make and do and create.
Will not the struggle to transform the world
make me live?

DEAD GOD OR DEAD MAN?

In the 19th Century the problem was that God was
dead; In the 20th Century the problem is that
man is dead.

Erich Fromm

This is death! The acceptance of things as they are.
How could a dead man want a live God?

LIVING SPRINGS FROM DYING

The reality witnessed to by the parables of Jesus is the reality of life moving toward fulfillment through crucifixion. They suggest that human fulfillment often is experienced not when we strive desperately after it, but when we are willing not to seek it because of a higher loyalty. We discover life when we allow our self-satisfaction to be challenged and our easy securities to be called into question; when we face the shattering of our neat presuppositions and systems, and then discover that each moment of death is really a new beginning.

Richard Shaull

How unsettling life with You can be. I always try to quit, to rest secure at some level of achievement; but You won't have it! I'd like to be able to contain You, to hold You to some fixed goal; but You break the boundries and force me ever forward. Why do I look back with longing, around with dismay, and not ahead with joy and excitement?

LEFT EMPTY

Time lost is time in which we have failed to live a human life, gain experience, learn, create, enjoy, and suffer; it is time that has been filled up, but left empty.

Dietrich Bonhoeffer

But we need not be discouraged. Is not what is empty capable of being filled full?

MARANATHA

Who is right: the exultant, joy-filled early Christians or the dour, straight-faced Puritans? And on whose side am I rooting? Do I see myself as a weighty spirit, loaded down with the self-important solemnity of the Puritans and Jansenists? Or am I still able to respond with something like the joyous spontaneity of the early Christians: Maranatha, **"Come, O Lord!"?**

Phil.

It is good to be reminded that
4:3 **our names are in the book of life.**
4 **I rejoice in you, O Lord, always; again I say to myself: "Rejoice"** . . .
5 **for you, my God, are at hand.**

6 **May we have no anxiety, but in everything by prayer and supplication with thanksgiving let our requests be made known to your Father.**
7 **So may the peace of God, which passes all understanding, keep our hearts and our minds in you, Christ Jesus.**

8 **Finally, whatever is true, whatever is honorable, whatever is just, whatever is pure, whatever is lovely, whatever is gracious— if there is any excellence, if there is anything worthy of praise—** may this be the argument of our thoughts;
9 **then your Father, the God of peace, will be with us.**
10 **I will rejoice in you, my Lord,** . . .
11 **and not complain of want** . . .

**In whatever state I am,
I will be content,**
for you are there with me.

12 **In any and all circumstances
I must learn the secret**
of facing plenty and hunger,
abundance and want.

13 **I can do all things in you
who strengthen me.**

19 And I firmly believe that **your divine Father
will supply every need of mine**
according to his riches
in you, Christ Jesus.

30 **To our God and Father be glory
for ever and ever. Amen.**

Paul Hilsdale

*We can do so much more, We can be so much
more. How many things can I still do that I have
as yet left undone?*

THE WAY

"(The Way of Mahayana) **is not a way of running
away from the world but of overcoming it
through growing knowledge** (Prajna) **through
active love** (Maitri) **towards ones fellow beings,
through inner participation in the joys and
sufferings of others** (Karuna, Mudita) **and through
equanimity** (Upeksa) **with regard to one's own
weal and woe."**

Foundations of Tibetan Mysticism

The way is open—am I?

QUESTIONING

**The men who create power make an indispensable
contribution to the nation's greatness, but the
men who question power make a contribution
just as indispensable, especially when that
questioning is disinterested, for they determine
whether we use power or power uses us. Our
national strength matters, but the spirit which
informs and controls our strength matters just
as much.**

John F. Kennedy

*The way of questioning, the way of searching—
are not these the ways to life? The answer,
the find—are not these a further invitation to life?*

THE PROCESS

**the entire human environment . . . a teaching
machine . . . to make everyday learning a process
of Discovery.**

Marshall McLuhan

*The area of search is large, the questions are many,
and the process will be never-ending, but this is
life—and have I lived enough?*

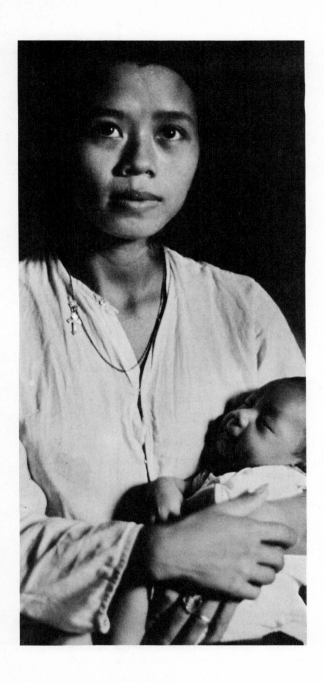

ST. PAUL'S PRAYER OF PRAISE

Praise be to the God the Father of our Lord
  Jesus Christ, who has blessed us
  with every spiritual blessing,
  with the heavenly realm
  with Christ.
Blessings
I For in him he chose us before the foundation
    of the world,
    to be holy
    and above reproach in his sight;
II out of love he destined us
    to become for him adoptive sons
      through Jesus Christ,
    —such was his will and pleasure—
  in view of the praise and glory of his gracious
    gift
  which he has bestowed on us in the Beloved.

III It is through union with him and through
    his blood
    that our redemption is achieved and
      our offenses forgiven,
    according to the abundance of his favor
    which he has lavished upon us, with
      all wisdom and understanding.

IV He has made known to us his hidden purpose
    and will,
    according to that design which he
    proposed to carry out in Christ,
      to realize it when the time would be
  ripe,
    that everything in heaven and on earth
    might be brought together under the
    headship of Christ—

V The Christ, in whom it is our lot to have
    been predestined
    (by the plan of him who realizes every-

thing according to his will and
purpose)
to be—for the praise of his glory—
the first to set our hope on Christ.

VI It is in union with him too that you,
who have heard the message of truth,
the good news of your salvation,
in which you have believed,
have been marked with the seal of the
promised Holy Spirit,
who is the pledge of what we shall
inherit,
in view of the redemption of God's
own possession,
in view of the praise of his glory.

Epistle To Ephesians
Chapter One: 3-14

Arranged in sense lines by J. A. Fitzmyer, S. J.

Your purpose and will, they are my future and my life. May I live and be and help to bring the earth to a ripened fullness.

BUILDING THE EARTH

The function of man
is to build and direct the whole of the earth.
Having lived for millennia in self-contradiction,
mankind has now reached a stage of development
from which it can,
with all its forces, advance forward.
It will be objected
that in order to finally constitute
a Crusade of Man,
there must be some "antagonist" to oppose.
For my part, I do not believe in the
supreme effectiveness of the instinct of preservation
and fear.
It is not the fear of perishing,
but the ambition to live
which has thrown man into the exploration
of nature,
the conquest of the atmosphere
and the heavens.
Until now, we have rightly been passionate
in seeking to unveil
the mysteries concealed in matter,
infinitely great and infinitesimally small mysteries.
But an inquiry
of much greater importance to the future
will be the study of psychic currents and attractions,
a science of spiritual energy.
Perhaps, impelled by the necessity to build
the unity of the World,
we shall end by perceiving that the great object
unconsciously pursued by science
is nothing else than the discovery of God.
Stimulated by consecutive discoveries
which in the space of a hundred years
have successively revealed to our generation several
important things
—first the profundities and significance of time,
then the limitless spiritual resources of matter,
and lastly the power of living beings acting in

association—
it seems that our psyche is in the process of
    changing.
A conquering passion which will sweep away or
    transform
what has hitherto been the immaturity of the earth
has begun to show itself,
And its salutary action
comes just at the right moment
to control, awaken, or order
the emancipated forces of love,
the dormant forces of human unity,
and the hesitant forces of research.
The whole question.
in this crisis of birth,
is the rapid emergence of the soul
which by its appearance will organize,
lighten and vitalize
this mass of stagnant and confused material.
But this soul can only be a "conspiracy"
of individuals who associate themselves
to raise to a new stage the edifice of life.

The resources we enjoy today,
the powers and secrets of science we have
    discovered,
cannot be absorbed by the narrow system
of individual and national divisions
which have so far served the leaders of the world.
The age of nations is past.
The task before us now, if we would not perish,
is to shake off our ancient prejudices, and to build
    the earth.
It has become fashionable today
to mock or to treat with suspicion
anything which looks like faith in the future.
If we are not careful
this skepticism will be fatal,
for its direct result
is to destroy
both the love of living

and the momentum of mankind.
Firmly based on the general history of the world,
as revealed to us by paleontology,
over a period of 300 million years,
we can make these two assertions,
without losing our foothold in dreams:
a) First and foremost,
mankind still shows signs of a reserve,
a formidable potential of concentration,
that is, of progress.
Think of the immensity
of the powers,
ideas
and persons
not yet discovered
or harnessed
or born
or synthesized.
In terms
of "energy"
and biology,
the human race is still very young and very fresh.
b) The earth is still far
from having completed
its sidereal evolution.
True,
we can imagine
all sorts of catastrophes
which might intervene
to cut short
this great development.

But for 300 million years now,
Life has been going on paradoxically
in the midst of improbability.
Does that not indicate
that it is marching forward,
sustained by some complicity
in the motive forces of the Universe?
The real dificulty

which faces man
is not the certainty
that he is the seat of constant progress;
it is rather the conception
of how this progress
can go on
for a long time yet at its present rate,
without life exploding itself
or blowing up the earth
on which it was born.
Our modern world
was created
in less than ten thousand years,
and in the last two hundred years
it has changed faster
than in all the previous millenia.

Progress,
if it is to continue,
will not happen by itself.
Evolution,
by the very mechanism
of its syntheses,
is constantly
acquiring greater freedom.
In practice,
what steps must we take
in relation to this forward march?

I see two,
which can be summarized in five words:
a great hope
in common.
a) First, a great hope.
This must be born spontaneously
in every generous soul
in face of the anticipated work,
and it also represents
the essential impetus
without which nothing

will be done.
A passionate love of growth,
and being,
that is what we need.
Down with the cowards and the skeptics,
the pessimists and the unhappy,
the weary and the stagnant.
b) In common.

On this point also
the history of Life
is decisive.
There is only one way
which leads upwards;
the one which,
through greater organization,
leads to greater
synthesis and unity.
Here again, then,
down with the pure individualists,
the egoists, who expect to grow by excluding
or diminishing their brothers
—individually, nationally
or racially.
Life is moving toward unification.
Our hope
will only be operative
if it is expressed
in greater cohesion
and human solidarity.
The future of the earth is in our hands.
How shall we decide?
A common science merely brings
the geometric point of
different intelligences
nearer together.
A common interest,
however passionate,
merely brings beings into indirect touch,
through an impersonal which destroys personality.

It is not our heads
or our bodies
which we must bring
together,
but our hearts.
The generating principle
of our unification
is not finally to be found
in the single contemplation
of the same truth
or in the single desire
awakened by something,
but in the single attraction
by the same
Someone.

The great event
which we are awaiting
(is) the discovery
of a synthetic act
of adoration
in which are allied
and mutually exalted
the passionate desire
to conquer
the world,
and the passionate desire
to unite ourselves
with God;
the vital act,
specifically new,
corresponding to a new age
of the earth.

Teilhard De Chardin

A visionary vista exposes itself to view, and a great challenge to man's freedom and purpose calls forth. But how will this new vision be made into reality? Your call, Father, must be heeded and the whole world built into an adoring unity of love. You ask us to be brave, to be happy and optimistic, and above all to be energetic and dynamic in building this new world of adoring unity. Nothing else will meet this challenge to our freedom, nothing else will make us more. Can I have this great hope? Can I bring it to and share it with all men?

HAPPINESS

I touch the color of your
alpha silence sounds
vigorous, warm, fresh
I smell the wind of kindness
in prayer of thought
escalating with frozen motion
in a brilliance of
quiet shouts of joy
to your sky
alive in you
a zoom lens of activity
creating voidless energy
for an instant of meaning
to hear
the multicolored sounds of
creativity
vision
omega word

Base your happiness on your hope in Christ. Give
freely to those in want. And as for those who try
to make your life a misery, bless them. Don't
curse, bless. Share the happiness of those that
are happy, and the sorrow of those that are sad.

Romans 12: 14-15

LITANY

My God, my God, why have you forsaken me?

For if You have, to whom shall I turn?

**You are far from my pleas and the words of my cry.
I call all day, my God, but you never answer; all
night long I call and cannot rest . . .**

*I really want to be happy in Your love and service,
but at times I do not know how—and even
when I do, I fail.*

**In you our fathers put their trust, they trusted and
you rescued them; they called to you for
help and they were saved . . .**

*I turn to You aware of Your wonderful works
in the past and aware of my present need. Are
you now active?*

**I am like water draining away, my bones are all
disjointed, my heart is like wax, melting inside
me; my palate is drier than a potsherd and my
      tongue
is stuck to my jaw.**

When I am down, I feel I can't go on.

**A pack of dogs surrounds me, a gang of villains
closes me in; they tie me hand and foot and
leave me lying in the dust of death.**

*I look for help but I find more adversaries—
even among my friends.*

**Do not stand aside, Yahweh.
Oh my strength, come quickly to my help!
Rescue my soul from the sword,
my dear life from the paw of the dog.
Save me from the lion's mouth,
my poor soul from the wild bull's horns!**

*My God, it's You I need. I have no other friend.
You hold out a vision for me and call me to it—will
You not be with me on the way?*

**Then shall I proclaim your name to my brothers,
praise you in full assembly:**

*When I am moving again confidently, happily
toward a better, more complete, more whole future.*

**You who fear Yahweh, praise him!
Entire race of Jacob, glorify him!
Entire race of Israel, revere him!**

All people, praise the God of our happy future!

**For he has not despised or disdained the poor man
in his poverty, has not hidden his face from him,
but has answered him when he called.**

I trust You, I hope in You—We can show them.

**Happy are the utterly sincere,
for they will see God**

Matthew 5: 8

*For I know that Your way of love, Your way of
freedom, Your way to life are the only way to a
happy future. Is it not the only way worthy of
all my work?*

**How happy are those who know
what sorrow means, for they
will be given courage and comfort**

Matthew 5: 4

Only if I can admit my need, will I feel Your power.

**Happy are those who claim
nothing for the whole earth
will belong to them.**

Matthew 5: 5

*Is it not my desire to cling to the present, to hold
onto the old that binds me down? Help me to
cut loose!*

**Happy are those who are
hungry and thirsty for
goodness, for they will be
fully satisfied.**

Matthew 5: 5

*The desire for justice and goodness and a new
future is the only desire that will liberate. Why
am I eager for other things?*

The essence of optimism is not its view of the present, but the fact that it is the inspiration of life and hope when others give in.

Dietrich Bonhoeffer

I know my present weakness, but I hope for our future. Is not this happiness?

May the brilliance of your light illumine the massive obscurities in which we move.

Teilhard De Chardin

I do not overlook the evils and failures of the present, but I look into them with Your light and see a future to work happily towards. What else could happiness be?

**Calm is the soul that is emptied of all self,
In a restful harmony—
This happiness is here and now,
A happiness within you–but not yours.**

Dag Hammarskjold

In the end, am I not tne obstacle to my own happiness? You call and You fulfill—but I must lose myself in You.

HE LIVES! HE LIVES!

The rocks cry out
and part in wonder
Sun beams
and throws out its arms
awaking the world
to glorious truth
HE LIVES!
Wind plays with petals
teasing, caressing
in mood so delightful
stirring the flowers
and grasses
and scurrying insects
to nature's own rhythm
HE LIVES!
Then man
who is master
of wind, rock and nature
joins heart, mind and voice
to earth's ringing gladness
His whole being looks out
and inward too
for new life
God's life
is quickening anew—
HE LIVES!

Sister Athena

And in Your life, I am happy.

ACKNOWLEDGMENTS

"Somehow I Didn't Know"
John Atherton, "somehow i didn't know," from
Motive Magazine (P.O. Box 871, Nashville,
Tenn. 37202), February, 1968. Reprinted by
permission.

"Tied Up"
Carl Burke, "Tied Up," *Treat Me Cool, Lord*,
New York: Association Press, 1968.

"All By Myself"
Carl Burke, "All by Myself," *Treat Me Cool, Lord*,
New York: Association Press, 1968.

"Jesus' Prayer"
Matthew Fox, "What is Prayer?," *Listening*,
Spring, 1968.

"Concerning Jesus of Nazareth"
Robert S. Jackson, "Concerning Jesus of Nazareth,"
from *Motive* Magazine (P.O. Box 871, Nashville,
Tenn. 37202), April, 1968.

"Genuinely for Others"
Bernard Cooke, S.J., *Christian Involvement*,
Argus Communications, Chicago, Ill. 60651.

"Love is Discovery"
Earnest Larsen, *Good Old Plastic Jesus*,
Liguorian Press.

"Community Improvisations"
"Community Improvisations," *The Bread Is
Rising, #4*, Emmaus House, New York, N.Y.

"The World Is Womb"
"The World Is Womb," *The Bread Is Rising, #4*,
Emmaus House, New York, N.Y.

"Conversations on Many Levels"
Corita Kent, "Choose Life," *The Living Light*,
Spring, 1966.

"Affirmation"
Dag Hammarskjold, *Markings,* © 1964, Alfred A.
Knopf, Inc., New York and Faber & Faber,
Ltd., London.

"Someplace"
Bill Jacobs, "Someplace," 1969, *The National
Denver Register,* Denver, Colorado.

"Prayer for the Morning Headlines"
Daniel Berrigan, S.J., "Prayer for the Morning
Headlines," *Love, Love at the End*. © 1968 by

Daniel Berrigan, S.J. The Macmillan Company,
New York, N.Y.

"Christianity and Community"
David Kirk, "Community as a Liberated Zone,"
The Bread Is Rising, #4, Emmaus House,
New York, N.Y.

"I See White and Black, Lord"
Malcolm Boyd, *Are You Running With Me, Jesus?*.
Copyright © 1965 by Malcolm Boyd. Reprinted
by permission of Holt, Rinehart and Winston, Inc.

"Letter from the Birmingham City Jail"
Martin Luther King, "Letter from the Birmingham
City Jail."

"Transforming the Profane"
Bernard Cooke, S.J., *Christian Involvement*,
Argus Communications, Chicago, Ill. 60651.

"We Live in Wonder"
Dag Hammarskjold, *Markings,* © 1964, Alfred A.
Knopf, Inc., New York and Faber & Faber,
Ltd., London.

"Who Am I?"
Dietrich Bonhoeffer, *The Cost of Discipleship*,
© 1960, The Macmillan Company, New York, N.Y.

**"My Legs Were Praying", "Saying Yes",
"Time to Create", "Contemplation"**
"Can Modern Man Pray?," *Time*, The Weekly
News Magazine, December 30, 1968. © Time, Inc.,
1968.

"Prologue of Saint John"
Translation by David Stanley, S.J.

"A Prayer for Making the Right Choices"
Carl Burke, "A Prayer for Making the Right
Choices," *Treat Me Cool, Lord*, New York:
Association Press, 1968.

"Prayer Is . . ."
Matthew Fox, "What is Prayer?," *Listening*,
Spring, 1968.

"Slow Down . . . Cool It"
Carl Burke, "Slow Down . . . Cool It," *Treat Me
Cool, Lord*, New York: Association Press, 1968.

"Rediscovery"
"Can Modern Man Pray?," *Time*, The Weekly News
Magazine, December 30, 1968 © Time, Inc., 1968.

"Touching Being Touched"
Richard Schaull, "The Political Significance of Parabolic Action," from *Motive* Magazine (P.O. Box 871, Nashville, Tenn. 37202), April, 1968. Reprinted by permission.

"The One Used Car That Was Snitched"
Carl Burke, "The One Used Car That Was Snitched," *God Is For Real, Man,* New York: Association Press, 1966.

"The Reality Is Christ"
"The Word of God and Prayer," *The Way,* Spring, 1967.

"A Parable"
Peter Fransen, *Divine Grace and Man,* 1962, Desclee and Sons, Publishers.

"A Contemplation"
"Contemplation for Achieving Love," *Spiritual Exercises of St. Ignatius,* P.J. Kenedy and Sons, New York, N.Y.

"Love's Powers"
Ross Snyder, "Love's Powers," *Inscape,* Copyright © 1968, by Abingdon Press, Nashville, Tennessee.

"Growth in You, O Lord"
Pierre Teilhard de Chardin, *The Divine Milieu.* Copyright © 1957 by Editions du Seuil, Paris. English translation copyright © 1960 by Wm. Collins Sons & Co., London, and Harper & Row, Publishers, Inc., New York.

"To Seek a Newer World"
Robert F. Kennedy, *To Seek a Newer World.* Copyright © 1967, 1968 by Robert F. Kennedy. Doubleday & Company, Inc., Publishers.

"This Is My Body"
Paul Hilsdale, *Prayers from St. Paul,* © 1964, Sheed & Ward, Inc.

"All You Need is Love"
Erich Fromm, *The Art of Loving.* Copyright © 1956, Harper & Row, Inc.

"Peace"
Robert W. Castle, Jr., *Prayers from the Burned-Out City,* © 1968, Sheed & Ward, Inc.

"Christian Involvement"
Bernard Cooke, S.J., *Christian Involvement,* Argus Communications, Chicago, Ill. 60651.

"Offer Your Gift"
Camilo Torres, translation by Virginia M. O'Grady, *Camilo Torres—His Life and His Message.* © Translation, 1968, Templegate Publishers.

"Jungle Games"
Robert Haiduke, "Jungle Games," © 1968 by Robert Haiduke. Reprinted by permission of the author.

"Unto Death"
Paul Hilsdale, *Prayers from St. Paul,* © 1964, Sheed & Ward, Inc.

"What Was Hiroshima Like, Jesus, When the Bomb Fell?"
Malcolm Boyd, *Are You Running With Me, Jesus?.* Copyright © 1965 by Malcolm Boyd. Reprinted by permission of Holt, Rinehart and Winston, Inc.

"Death is a Button"
Motive Magazine (P.O. Box 871, Nashville, Tenn. 37202), February, 1968. Reprinted by permission.

"Sequeiros' Echo of a Scream"
Thomas R. Heath, O.P., "Sequeiros' Echo of a Scream." Reprinted by permission of the author.

"Contemplative Life"
Thomas Merton, "Contemplative Life," *Commonweal,* July 4, 1947.

"Napalm"
Robert Haiduke, "Napalm," © 1968 by Robert Haiduke. Reprinted by permission of the author.

"God's Presence"
Carl Burke, "God's Presence," *Treat Me Cool, Lord,* New York: Association Press, 1968.

"A Prayer of Discipleship"
Malcolm Boyd, *Are You Running With Me, Jesus?.* Copyright © 1965 by Malcolm Boyd. Reprinted by permission of Holt, Rinehart and Winston, Inc.

"A Psalm for the New Humanity"
Nancy Gallagher, "A Psalm for the New Humanity," *New City,* October, 1967.

"By Their Vegetables Shall You Know Them"
"By Their Vegetables Shall You Know Them," *New City,* June, 1968.

"The Meaning of Religion"
Paul Hilsdale, *Prayers from St. Paul,* © 1964, Sheed & Ward, Inc.